PRAISE F
WALT DISNEY WORLD HACKS

"I don't care how many times you've been to Walt Disney World; *Walt Disney World Hacks* has a bunch of tips you've never thought of. This easy-to-read book is a must-have for those planning their first trip, and a great read for those who think they already know it all. In addition to Walt Disney World tips, you'll find lots of hacks you can use at Disneyland and other theme parks, as well as many general travel tips."
—Matt Roseboom, *Attractions Magazine*

"Booking and navigating a Walt Disney World vacation is more complex than ever, especially for new and occasional park visitors. Susan Veness has written a book with an abundance of tips to help make that process easier. I recommend highlighting tips of interest ahead of time and carrying the book with you for easy reference."
—Denise Preskitt and Jeff Lange, MouseSteps.com

"Susan Veness can help you avoid many of the headaches and hassles that typically trip up travelers who are Orlando bound. The smart insider tips you'll uncover while reading *Walt Disney World Hacks* are sure to make your visit to Walt Disney World's theme parks that much more enjoyable."
—Jim Hill, *Disney Dish* podcast

"Must-have secrets for the perfect Disney World vacation!"
—John Frost, *The Disney Blog*

Walt Disney World
HACKS

2ND EDITION

Susan Veness
with Samantha Davis-Friedman

Adams Media

New York London Toronto Sydney New Delhi

A adamsmedia

Adams Media
An Imprint of Simon & Schuster, LLC
100 Technology Center Drive
Stoughton, Massachusetts 02072

This Adams Media trade paperback edition April 2024
First Adams Media trade paperback edition April 2019

ADAMS MEDIA and colophon are registered trademarks of Simon & Schuster, LLC.

Simon & Schuster: Celebrating 100 Years of Publishing in 2024

For information about special discounts for bulk purchases, please contact Simon & Schuster Special Sales at 1-866-506-1949 or business@simonandschuster.com.

The Simon & Schuster Speakers Bureau can bring authors to your live event. For more information or to book an event, contact the Simon & Schuster Speakers Bureau at 1-866-248-3049 or visit our website at www.simonspeakers.com.

Interior design by Michelle Kelly
Interior images © iStockphoto.com; 123RF
Interior maps by Eric Andrews; © Simon & Schuster, LLC

Manufactured in the United States of America

1 2024

Library of Congress Cataloging-in-Publication Data
Names: Veness, Susan, author. | Davis-Friedman, Samantha, author.
Title: Walt Disney World hacks, 2nd edition / Susan Veness, with Samantha Davis-Friedman.
Other titles: Three hundred fifty plus park secrets for making the most of your Walt Disney World vacation
Description: 2nd edition, 1st Adams Media trade paperback edition. | Stoughton, Massachusetts: Adams Media, [2024] | Series: Disney hidden magic gift series | Previous edition published: 2019.
Identifiers: LCCN 2023049262 | ISBN 9781507221952 (pb) | ISBN 9781507221969 (ebook)
Subjects: LCSH: Walt Disney World (Fla.)--Guidebooks.
Classification: LCC GV1853.3.F62 V47 2024 | DDC 791.06/875924--dc23/eng/20231026
LC record available at https://lccn.loc.gov/2023049262

ISBN 978-1-5072-2195-2
ISBN 978-1-5072-2196-9 (ebook)

ACKNOWLEDGMENTS

I would like to thank my contributing writer, Samantha Davis-Friedman, for all her help, and for the fun Disney banter we've had over the past few years.

Thank you to Matt Roseboom, publisher of the excellent *Attractions Magazine* theme park news and information resource.

And a heartfelt thanks to my superb editor, Julia Belkas, who makes all of my work better.

CONTENTS

INTRODUCTION

Few vacation destinations are as magical as Walt Disney World, and few require as much advance planning, especially as Disney becomes more dependent on technology. Between figuring out which theme park tickets to purchase, how to use Genie+ and Lightning Lane, where you'll dine, and how to keep everyone from having a major meltdown in the middle of Main Street U.S.A., it can be an exercise in frustration if you're not prepared with shortcuts and sanity-saving insights.

That's where *Walt Disney World Hacks, 2nd Edition* comes in, teaching you tips and tricks that will smooth the path and lead to magical memories. Even those who "wing it" will benefit from a few good hacks that will help make the most of their visit.

Throughout the book, watch for "Newbie" and "Pro" hacks geared toward each level of proficiency, take note of the Practical Matters hacks to avoid common frustrations, and master the intricacies of working within Disney's systems to make the most of your time and your money. Learn secrets to get savings on the paid-for Genie+ and Individual Lightning Lane; become Disney-discounts savvy; discover ways to enjoy rides and attractions without the long waits; and, if you're visiting with children, find out how yours can be the family with a genuine smile on everyone's face from park opening to park closing.

From the early planning stages to traveling to Orlando, scoring the best dining, when to experience the most popular attractions, and softening the logistics of returning home, each aspect of your Disney vacation is covered. And, when you're ready to book a return trip to the most magical place on Earth, there are hacks for that too!

CHAPTER 1

YOU'RE GOING TO WALT DISNEY WORLD!

1.
Prioritize Attractions Wisely

There are a limited number of E-Ticket attractions that everyone wants to ride, so be sure to prioritize which rides are your "must dos" and which are "can waits." That way, you'll know which attraction to select first if you've purchased Disney Genie+ or where to head first when you get through the gates. If you're an early riser and can get to the parks when they open, you may even be able to knock out a few top picks early in the day and save rides with shorter wait times for later. This strategy is particularly useful in Pandora–The World of Avatar at Animal Kingdom or Star Wars: Galaxy's Edge at Hollywood Studios, which both boast high-demand attractions. Disney Genie can also help. If you set your "Genie Day" in the My Disney Experience app for *only* your first-choice attraction, that will push it to the top of your Tip Board, which means you won't have to scroll to find it, saving precious seconds when securing a Lightning Lane return time.

2.
Get to Know Disney Genie

Even before you travel to Orlando, it's a good idea to familiarize yourself with the Disney Genie service in the My Disney Experience app. This complimentary planning tool helps maximize time in the parks by tracking wait times and making recommendations based on the attractions, shows, and experiences you prioritize. Just click the "My Day" tab and follow the prompts to make your choices. For an additional fee per person per day, the Disney Genie+ service offers expedited entry for certain attractions on a rolling basis throughout the day—known as Lightning Lane, but previously as FastPass+. Additional attractions (usually the most popular ride in each park) offer separately purchased Individual Lightning Lane return times. You do not need Genie+ to purchase Individual Lightning Lane, but those rides are not available through Genie+. If you choose neither paid option, Standby queues are available for most attractions, and Genie will still alert you when wait times are low.

3.
Budget-Friendly Genie+ Pricing

The price for Genie+ varies from day-to-day and from park-to-park. Single-park ticket holders can purchase Genie+ for only that park. If you have a Park Hopper ticket, you can pay one price for Genie+ service at all four theme parks throughout your stay, but if you only plan to visit one park on any given day, purchasing Genie+ for only that park is a budget-friendly idea. You can purchase Genie+ beginning at midnight on the date you plan to visit.

4.
Understand Virtual Queue

Modern technology also comes into play at Walt Disney World in the form of virtual queues. This "first come, first served" system is often implemented for the newest/highest-demand attractions and can be accessed through the My Disney Experience app. Think of it as a lottery system: Park guests request to join a virtual queue at a specified time of day (usually offered once in the morning and once in the afternoon), but may not "win" a spot. Frequent parkgoers claim there are "tricks" to snagging a virtual queue, but like a lottery, it's just a matter of luck—and even if you get lucky, there's no guarantee you'll ride because breakdowns usually equal backlogs. When a virtual queue is in place for an attraction, a Standby queue will not be available, but sometimes Lightning Lane reservations are offered through Genie+. Virtual queues are available at 7 a.m. and 1 p.m., and they go fast, so plan accordingly.

5.
Power Up Your Cell Phone

Your cell phone will get a lot of use while you're playing in the theme parks. You'll use it to mobile-order food via the My Disney Experience app, and to check your restaurant reservation times and booking numbers (or to make or cancel reservations if your plans change). You'll also use it to check your Genie+ selections or change your selections on the go. While Disney's Wi-Fi is generally reliable, the one thing that is likely to give out is your phone's battery. Bring along a portable power bank to charge it as you tour rather than fight for one of the few charging stations in the park. You can even find solar-powered chargers, perfect for use in the Sunshine State. Disney also offers FuelRods (for a fee) which can be exchanged for a fully-charged rod when the first one runs out. FuelRods can also be purchased from Amazon before your trip.

6.
Finger Scan or ID

Gone are the days of turnstiles at Disney's theme park front gates. In their place are scanners that read guests' entry tickets or MagicBands, and the fingerprint connected to each person's park admission. But what if you're not comfortable with biometric scans? No problem. Although the scanners turn each fingerprint image into a "numerical value" and discard the image rather than entering it into a database, you don't have to use the system to enter the parks. Simply show photo identification, such as a driver's license or passport, which corresponds with the name on your park pass or MagicBand, and you're good to go. Take note: You'll need your photo ID each time you enter a park.

7.
Newbie Alert: Plan in Order

Following a timeline for your bookings makes planning a first-time visit less overwhelming. First, book your flights. Next, book your resort. Also, purchase park passes and make your theme park reservations (if needed) at that time. Then, book a rental car, if you're using one (or airport transfers if you're not). At 180 days prior to travel, start booking dining reservations, dinner shows you'd like to see, and other experiences such as tours or a visit to Bibbidi Bobbidi Boutique.

8.
Get Dressy

Victoria & Albert's at Disney's Grand Floridian Resort & Spa boasts Forbes Travel Guide's prestigious Five-Star Award and has been awarded the AAA Five Diamond designation every year since 2000. As would be expected at such an elegant venue, the dress code requires men to wear a shirt with a collar. To keep the collar from getting crushed in your suitcase while you're in transit, coil the belt you'll be wearing with your dress slacks and insert it into the collar of the folded shirt. Tension from the belt will keep the collar upright, and the belt's edge will hold up any clothes placed on top of it. For extra padding, stuff your dress socks into the empty space inside the coiled belt.

9.
Have a Park-Free First Day

Orlando vacations often start with an arrival at midday or later due to long car rides or flight schedules, which means getting less than full value from that day's theme park admission. Make the most of a late arrival by purchasing one less day on your tickets and do what Walt Disney did when choosing land for his Florida parks: Put a "buffer zone" between the real world and the theme parks, and make your first day a laid-back transition day. Settle into your resort, enjoy the pool, and head to Disney Springs Guest Services if you need to exchange eTickets for hard tickets. Your first evening is also ideal for a character meal where you can meet your favorites without a long, hot wait in the parks.

10.
Write Down Your Schedule

The new reality at Walt Disney World is that you'll be connected to your phone throughout the day. If you prefer not to let technology take over your vacation, print out a small daily spreadsheet, highlighting your Genie+ bookings and any restaurant reservations you've made, and have it laminated so it's waterproof. Or use the "poor man's lamination" trick by laying strips of clear packing tape sticky-side up on a table, press your spreadsheet onto it, cover it with more tape, and cut it down to size. Be sure to round the edges so they don't poke you when reaching for it in your backpack. Crafty? Punch a hole in one corner and hang it on your backpack using a carabiner or book binder ring.

11.
Photograph Your Schedule

To avoid having to open the My Disney Experience app on your phone each time you need to check your Genie+ or dining reservation times, write down a daily schedule with all the important times and locations on a white piece of paper, with each day's date at the top. Take a separate photo of each schedule using your cell phone, and the info will be readily at hand, even if you enter one of the dreaded Wi-Fi drop-out zones around the parks, or when Disney's Wi-Fi system goes down, which does happen occasionally. Remember not to delete your schedule photos if you download your gallery on an Android phone or Photos on iPhone, but do delete them at the end of each day to avoid any confusion.

12.
Create Your Own Thank-You Cards

Before you leave home, decorate several index cards, using stickers or drawing with markers, to carry in your backpack while you're in the theme parks. Write things like, "Thank you for making my day magical," "Sprinkling you with pixie dust to thank you for all you do," "You're the real magic in the most magical place on Earth," and "Thank you for going above and beyond." Be sure to sign them with your name or "From the _____ Family." Allow kids to hand out their own cards as a reminder to be grateful to others. Even easier, enter the phrase "Printable Disney Cast Member thank-you cards" or "Cast Member appreciation cards" into a search engine for several websites that offer templates for free.

Plan a Surprise Vacation

The only thing more fun than planning a Walt Disney World vacation is surprising someone with a Walt Disney World vacation. Whether you're keeping it a secret from the kids until you're already in transit, or it's a January birthday gift for a December trip, the moment of your grand reveal can be unforgettable.

13. **First, consider the receiver.** Think carefully about how and when they'd like to be told. Some people love surprises; some like to be in on the decision-making and enjoy the anticipation of a countdown. If you're planning a summer trip, Christmas or Hanukkah may be too soon to tell preschoolers but ideal for teens, so tailor your "reveal" to their personality for the best response.

14. **For an easy and inexpensive reveal,** fill a wrapped box with Disney character helium balloons tied to a note from "Mickey," or wrap up a travel outfit with a T-shirt featuring the person's favorite Disney character and leave it on their bed on departure morning.

15. **Kids love scavenger hunts.** Create clues based on a Disney character or movie and hide them in corresponding locations, such as "#1. Where in our living room would Pluto sleep?" with the next clue hidden under the dog's bed.

16. **Have a Disney movie night, then surprise everyone with custom-made T-shirts,** such as, "Jimmy Jones. I'm Going to Walt Disney World!" It isn't a given, but guests wearing matching T-shirts are often chosen to ride in the Magic Kingdom parade.

17. **Cut out yellow construction paper footprints shaped like Mickey's shoe,** and have them lead up to your reveal. Strew Mickey confetti over a table with filled vacation backpacks and your MagicBands.

18. **Tuck a Disney Gift Card into the toe of a Christmas stocking.** Add a note stating, "Here is $50 to spend at Walt Disney World!" Or slip a new autograph book and a fat pen into the stocking, with the reveal on the front page.

19. **Mail a "Secret Mission" to older kids or teens, featuring elaborate clues and difficult puzzles,** with the big reveal at the end. Take a page out of the Disney Imagineers' handbook and create a detailed backstory, then play along as if you're part of the mission so that you can drop hints if the clues prove too difficult.

20. **Want to do a treasure hunt? Crumple up a big piece of white paper;** steep it in cold, strong-brewed tea; let it dry; draw your map on it; then singe the edges a bit. Hide clues to the big reveal around the house or yard, leading treasure hunters to an X-marks-the-spot. Bury a small treasure chest with the final clue, and be sure to leave a shovel nearby for digging.

21. **For a last-minute reveal,** create a treasure hunt with clues attached to items the surprisee will use during the trip, with a packed suitcase and a pair of Mickey ears as the "treasure." Then, tell them it's time to go!

Don't forget to video the moment. Your "reveal" may be the next social media sensation.

22.
Share the Light

While you're at the dollar store purchasing light-up toys for yourself or your kids (see Chapter 2), splurge on a few more to hand out to other children during long waits for nighttime parades, fireworks, or shows such as Fantasmic! at Disney's Hollywood Studios, the seasonal Tree of Life Awakenings at Disney's Animal Kingdom, or Happily Ever After at Magic Kingdom. Kids with light-up items will feel like they are part of the show, and it's a magical way to end the day, especially when you share it with others.

23.
Newbie Alert: Take a Midday Break

When you've paid all that money for a vacation with Mickey and friends, the very idea of not squeezing every penny out of it seems unthinkable. However, while taking a midday break each day, or every other day, during your stay is the most counterintuitive thing you can do, it's also the one decision you'll sing the praises of when you return home. By planning for time out of the parks at midday, you'll escape the worst of the heat and humidity as well as avoid lines when they are at their longest. Not only that, but the parks are at their most magical at night, and you won't burn out before the fireworks begin.

24.
Anticipate the "Day Three" Phenomenon

The average guest is filled with adrenaline for the first two days of his vacation. He's up by 7 a.m., he's had breakfast, and he's chomping at the bit to get into the parks for opening time. By the third day, especially in summertime when Florida's heat and humidity can be exhausting, you'll be lucky to have your teeth brushed by 11 a.m. Bear that in mind when making any bookings in advance, opting for time slots of 11:30 a.m. and later starting on your third day. However, if you want to use Genie+, or hope to secure one of the "hard to get" Individual Lightning Lane attractions, get up early to make your selections, then head back to bed for another hour or two!

25.
Disney Box

Many first-time visitors think their Disney vacation will be a one-off "trip of a lifetime," but when they return home, they're ready to book the next one. Keeping track of the accoutrements can be difficult, and that's where a Disney box comes in. Create a dedicated box to store autograph books, Sharpie markers, MagicBands, rain ponchos, refillable mugs or water bottles, misting fans, Disney trading pins, and other essentials you'll want to take with you each time you visit. Having them all in one place saves you from having to purchase basics again because you left them at home. Be sure to include less obvious items such as lanyards, moleskin pads, and carabiners, which are easy to forget.

26.

Create Personalized Honeymoon Keepsakes

There is no mistaking a honeymooner at Disney. Although bride-and-groom Mouse Ears are timeless attention-getters in the parks, personalized items add to the "happily ever after" sentiment once you're home again. Choose an ornament at Disney's Days of Christmas in Disney Springs and have it personalized by an on-site artist, then add new ones during return visits; in the theme parks or at Disney Springs, select hand-drawn sketches of the characters that most represent each of you, and have them personalized and signed by the artist; sit for a couples' silhouette, portrait, or caricature; or purchase hand-engraved, personalized wine or champagne glasses at Magic Kingdom, EPCOT, or Disney Springs. They're everlasting, just like love.

27.

Newbie Alert: Prepare to "Go with the Flow"

If you are holding multiday Park Hopper tickets and plan to use Disney's Genie+ queue-beating system, compare each day's pricing for "single-park" and "multiple parks." Even if you visit just two parks on any given day, it's less expensive to purchase the Genie+ multipark option. Unless you're absolutely certain you'll spend all day in one park on any given day, plans can change quickly during a Disney vacation and you'll have the flexibility to "go with the flow."

28.
Show Up for the Christmas Parade in November

The Christmas Day Parade is Disney's most nostalgic event, but if you show up on December 25 hoping to be a part of it, you're in for a disappointment. Taping takes place during the first week in November, with segments shot in select parks as well as Magic Kingdom each day, and the general public is only allowed into on-screen areas if space allows. Be aware: With all the reshooting of scenes, re-singing of songs, and relentless, crushing crowds, attending a taping is far less magical than seeing the parade on television. It's also a bucket list experience for die-hard fans, so don your Christmas garb, arrive well before park opening, steel yourself for a long, hot day, and be a part of the Yuletide joy!

29.
Take a School-Time Vacation

To avoid the heat, crowds, and high prices of a summer vacation, many parents choose to take their children to Disney during term time. Teachers may send along assignments, but with or without schoolwork, Disney is filled with ways to support learning if you take time to plan. Park maps reinforce directional skills and critical thinking; EPCOT's World Showcase is ideal for cultural and culinary experiences, and historical discussions; Magic Kingdom is filled with classic children's literature references (read the books first and discuss them while you're touring); and Wilderness Explorers at Animal Kingdom features free science and nature activities, while knowledgeable animal keepers are always on hand. Many attractions, especially at EPCOT, are filled with history, science, geography, and even oceanography lessons, but fun-while-learning opportunities are everywhere!

How to Use
My Disney Experience

Once you create a My Disney Experience account, click on "My Reservations" to link your resort reservation, link your family (and/or friends), then link tickets and customize MagicBands when prompted. Up to 180 days before your visit, go to "Make Dining Reservation" and select your choices. Finally, during your visit, choose other guests in your party and select your park and date each day. Know in advance which attractions you want, then select them from the list. Look for specific Genie+ and Individual Lightning Lane hacks throughout this book.

30.
Save for Disney

Most visitors to the House of Mouse save for a year or more to pay for "big ticket" items such as flights, accommodations, meals, and theme park admission. While you're setting aside larger sums each month, you can also save for smaller expenditures, such as souvenirs or ice cream. Create a "Disney money" jar or sealed box and drop your change into it after paying for items in cash. Set small goals, such as healthy daily eating to drop those ten pounds you've been meaning to get rid of, or, for kids, getting homework done without being told, and add a dollar to your stash each time you meet them, or penalize yourself by $5 each time you miss them. Even small change adds up quickly.

31.
Newbie Alert: You Can't Do It All

Walt Disney World is enormous. The theme parks alone boast nearly one hundred major shows and attractions, plus a wealth of other diversions, and that's before you add in the water parks, resorts, and Disney Springs. You can't do it all in a week, or even two weeks, so it's important to prioritize. As far in advance as possible, sit down with your family or fellow travelers and choose your top three attraction priorities for each day. Make those your Genie+ selections. Choose your next three priorities and mark them for additional Genie+ selections, or the next three attractions you'll visit. As you narrow down your priorities, that overwhelmed, chaotic feeling you're having will turn into a workable daily schedule.

32.
Celebrate Christmas Without the Crowds

The weeks surrounding Christmas and New Year's truly are the most magical, but they're also the busiest time of the year to visit Orlando. Visitors who want all of the magic without any of the crowds, take heart: Disney loves holidays so much, they start celebrating in November. Mickey's Very Merry Christmas Party starts the first week in November, EPCOT's International Festival of the Holidays begins in mid-November, and all of the Christmas decorations are up by mid-November too. The ICE! indoor "winter wonderland" Christmas events at nearby Gaylord Palms Resort also begin in mid-November; while Now Snowing, in the Disney-created town of Celebration, begins in late November. Book your vacation between November 8 and December 15 and enjoy Orlando's festive season with elbow room to spare.

Disney Genie and Genie+ Overview

Every guest visiting Walt Disney World is entitled to use the free Genie system, and the paid-for Genie+ and Individual Lightning Lane system, which allows you to avoid waiting in long lines. Here are the basics:

33. **Together or individually, the complimentary Genie and paid Genie+ services can help you get the most out of your Walt Disney World visit.** It's worth taking the time to enter your party's priorities so Genie can generate a personalized itinerary, based on what you entered, and map out your visit (including real-time updates). Genie can even suggest the best time to go to an experience or remind you when you're eligible to make dining and activity reservations so you don't miss a thing.

34. **Genie's custom Tip Board is a great resource that estimates wait times for your top attractions, entertainment, and dining.** You can also use it to order food via mobile ordering, make dining reservations, and check in to a restaurant.

35. **Most Lightning Lane entrances are offered through the Disney Genie+ service,** but others may be purchased individually (à la carte). You can purchase either Genie+ or Individual Lightning Lane—or both! Genie+ and Individual Lightning Lane prices vary by date, but are always priced per person, so for longer stays, you may decide you don't need them on every day of your vacation.

36. **Walt Disney World notes that guests can enter an average of two to three attractions or experiences per day via Lightning Lane entrances if the first selection is made early in the day,** but Lightning Lane entrances may be more difficult to reserve when the parks are crowded. On the other hand, if you visit at a less popular time of year, you will likely be able to ride more.

37. You can only use a Genie+ Lightning Lane entrance once per attraction, per day, so plan accordingly and track wait times. You'll make the most of your Genie+ purchase if you use it when waits are at their peak, and then use regular Standby lines for repeat rides when wait times are low. Disney states that guests will typically be able to use Lightning Lanes for two or three attractions per day but often you can get more than that if you plan wisely. You can enter a Lightning Lane five minutes before your Genie+ return time window opens and up to fifteen minutes after the window closes (and you can snag a new reservation as soon as you scan into the queue).

38. You can purchase Disney Genie+ service starting at midnight on the day of your park visit and make your first selection for Lightning Lane entry starting at 7 a.m. After that, selections can only be made one at a time. Once you enter the Lightning Lane queue or wait two hours (whichever comes first), you can make another selection. The fine print: The two-hour wait begins when the park opens, even if you made your first booking at 7 a.m.

39. Because there are many ways of touring the theme parks, there are also numerous strategies for working with the Genie and Genie+ systems. The way you use them will depend on the makeup of your group, whether you're staying on-site or off-site, if you're a Walt Disney World "newbie," whether you're an early riser or late sleeper, and even the time of year you're visiting. With that in mind, you'll find several more strategy hacks in Chapters 5 and 6.

40.
Choose a Hard Ticket or eTicket

When purchasing park passes online, you will often be given the choice of having them mailed to your home or receiving an eTicket in your email. There are pros and cons to each choice, so how does a vacationer decide? Check the seller's refund policy in the FAQ or Terms and Conditions. Some allow refunds on "hard tickets" (tickets that have been mailed to you), as long as they are not linked to your My Disney Experience account, but do not allow refunds on eTickets. Take note: Refunds are not allowed on any tickets purchased directly through Disney. Then, consider the time factor. You must stand in the line at will call to redeem eTickets, but can go straight to the gates with hard tickets.

41.
Be a Clothes-Folding Pro

You've passed the 180-day milestone for booking dining reservations. Nine days before you travel, you get to start doing the "single-digits dance." Three days before you travel, it's finally time to start packing, and that's when it occurs to you just how much stuff you have to fit into your suitcases. The way you fold your clothes—or rather, don't fold them—will determine how much space you have. Instead of folding shirts, shorts, and dresses, roll them. Stuff socks, underwear, and charging cables into shoes. You'll fit far more into your case. Want to become a true packing pro? Check out clothes-rolling tutorials or the KonMari Folding Method on YouTube.

42.
Newbie Alert: Special Events and Early Closings

You're enjoying a fun-filled day in Magic Kingdom, and every last detail is going right. Then, suddenly, bam! You discover the day you planned so carefully will end early due to a special event or a private party. Avoid this unhappy surprise by checking Disney's Special Events calendar at https://disneyworld.disney.go.com/calendars/day/#/animal-kingdom,hollywood-studios,epcot,magic-kingdom/ and using the Change Date feature as needed for a heads-up on any annual events, then check park hours at https://disneyworld.disney.go.com several months before you travel, while you're still sketching out your itinerary. Click on the "Parks & Tickets" drop-down menu, then on "More Hours" under "Park Hours." Reconfirm park closing hours closer to your arrival. Parks can close as early as 4:30 p.m. for private events, and if an unexpected early closing is listed, you'll still have time to change your plans.

43.
Check Your My Disney Countdown

Making your dining reservations at the 180-day mark sounds great, until you have to count 180 days on your calendar. If you're staying on-site, don't waste time tallying days the hard way. Once you have your Disney resort reservation linked to your My Disney Experience account, take a look at the "Welcome" banner at the top of the page. You'll see a calendar near your name that indicates how many days are left before your trip. A few days before the 180 mark, set an alert on your phone or computer (use your calendar if you're old school!) for 6 a.m. on the day or days you can make your dining reservations.

Understanding Disney's Ticket Pricing

There are a few things to keep in mind as you're shopping for Disney park admission. Ticket pricing is based on seasonal fluctuations, rising in high season and lowering when attendance is lighter. There are no discounts on single-day tickets, and purchasing any ticket at the gate is always most expensive. Multiday ticket pricing goes down per day the more days you add, with the biggest per-day price reductions on multiday tickets of five or more days. A standard theme park ticket includes admission to one theme park per day. For an additional cost, you can add a Park Hopper option, which allows you to visit more than one theme park on the same day. If theme park reservations are required, you must make the reservation for the first park you plan to visit each day.

44.

Pro Alert: Use Disney Gift Cards Wisely

One of the best questions is, "What do you want for your birthday," or anniversary, or any celebration, because the answer can be, "A Disney Gift Card." Most stores selling gift cards carry them, or you can purchase them online, but be sure to use your card wisely. Disney Gift Cards can only be used for purchases made directly through Disney, so before you pay for your Disney resort or tickets with your gift card, check for better discounts through booking outlets other than Disney. Instead, use your Disney Gift Card for on-site dining and merchandise purchases made on your MagicBand. A big bonus? They can also be used at Disney's Character Warehouse outlet stores.

45.
Condense Your Disney Gift Cards

Have several Disney gift cards with small balances? You can combine them all onto one gift card at DisneyGiftCard.com, but keep in mind that loading one card with a lot of money might not be the best idea for younger kids who want to carry their own card.

46.
Upgrade Base Tickets

You've purchased a resort and ticket package through Disney, but your group has different ideas when it comes to visiting more than one park per day. Grandparents don't want to "park hop" while the rest of the family does, or teens may want to hop when parents prefer not to, but all package tickets must be the same. What's a family to do? Opt for Base Tickets on the package, then, after check-in at your resort, upgrade to Park Hoppers for the people in your group who want to hop. Your tickets will become "separate" once you've checked in, and upgrading is possible. You must upgrade for the duration of the ticket, so make changes starting on your first day.

47.
Bring Out the Non-Disney Gift Cards

Those general-purpose gift cards you received as a gift or were given as a sign-up incentive by a company can be a bit of a pain. They aren't accepted everywhere, and you can end up with an odd balance after first use. All Disney locations accept them, regardless of the balance, so bring them along. Have five cards, each with a balance of a dollar or less? No problem! Scan away until their balances total zero, and pay any remaining balance with cash or your credit card or debit card. You can even make transactions the same way at the food and beverage kiosks during EPCOT's festivals.

48.
Practice Using Your Mobile App

You've studied how to select your Genie+ return times and how to mobile order to avoid waiting in quick-service queues. Now you're standing in a theme park with your My Disney Experience app open, and it's all gone haywire. You can't seem to find anything, let alone use it. There is no easy way around this once you're there, but you can avoid massive frustration by taking time to practice using your mobile app before you leave home. It isn't the most intuitive system ever invented, but once you know how to navigate, it will become second nature. And the good news is, you can always stop at a guest services kiosk located throughout the parks and ask Cast Members for help.

49.
Prep Your Cell Phone

Chances are you'll use your cell phone more during a Disney day than you do any other day of the year. Before you photograph your schedule and reservations to avoid opening your app and using your battery, remove photos and videos from your gallery, delete apps you don't use, turn off notifications, turn on low-power mode, and dim your screen. To save battery once you've arrived, turn off Wi-Fi and disable Location until you need to access your My Disney Experience app. Put your phone on airplane mode if you don't have to make or receive calls, and close apps after you use them. If your family has more than one phone, turn one on, then switch to the next phone when its battery runs out.

50.
Plan a Group "Reunion"

The only vacation better than a vacation with extended family or friends is a vacation without extended family or friends. While some of the best memories come from times the whole group is together, different styles of touring the parks can lead to silent resentment, or worse. Sit down as a group well in advance, and share honest expectations. It is often better to split up for all or part of a day, then reunite for dinner and share your experiences, than it is to force everyone to conform to one schedule.

CHAPTER 2

DISNEY FOR LESS

51.
When Not to Use Genie+

Genie+ can save a tremendous amount of time waiting in line, freeing you up to enjoy even more attractions. However, the extra cost may not fit comfortably within your budget. Consider skipping Genie+ if you're visiting during slower seasons, such as January, February, and November (unless there's a national holiday during your stay); you're staying for several days, you have Park Hopper tickets, and you can split up each park's attractions over the course of multiple early mornings and late evenings; or you or your group are willing to use the Single Rider line at attractions that offer it. Another option is to purchase Genie+ for your favorite park (or for Magic Kingdom, which benefits most from the system) for one day only.

52.
Take Advantage of Off-Season Discounts

The best way to immerse yourself in the Disney magic 24/7 is by staying at an on-site resort. Periodic discounts are offered year-round, but the most reliable savings on resort rooms are the off-season discounts. Once upon a time, "slow seasons" were obvious at Walt Disney World. Now, there is no true off-season, but crowds do lessen during some months, and booking discount incentives are more predictable. If you are able to travel between January 4 and mid-April (avoiding holidays and Spring Break), start looking for big general-public discount offers in early October. If you can travel in early August through early October, start looking for discounts in late April. Florida residents and Annual Passholders will reap the greatest rewards with off-season discounts.

53.
Grab Those Unique Offer Codes

You've scrimped and saved, but a Disney vacation remains just out of reach. Or you're considering a Disney trip, but you're holding back. You're the ideal target for a Unique Offer Code, an exclusive discount so dramatic there is no way you're not going to snap it up, pronto. Potential guests who have shown an interest, but repeatedly resist booking, might—just might—receive a coveted Unique Offer Code (first-timers, that means you). To maximize your chances, sign up for multiple (but accurate) Disney accounts, check "Special Offers" often, order a free planning video, and repeatedly utilize Disney's online reservations without booking. In short, leave an algorithm trail showing you need a final incentive. Be sure to accept communications via mail and email during sign-ups.

54.
Estimate Your Costs

The best way to plan a Disney vacation on a budget is to know what the basics cost, and plan your negotiables and nonnegotiables from there. Flights vary widely, but figuring out a rough estimate for the remainder of your trip is possible. In off-season, estimate non-Disney budget hotels at $75 to $100 per night, or Disney Value hotels at around $200 per night. Plan on paying roughly $15 per adult for counter-service meals; $10 each for kids' meals; $30 per day for parking ($45–$55 for preferred parking); and approximately $100 per day for an adult five-day Base Ticket and $90 per day for children. Guests only have to pay once to park each day, so be sure to keep your receipt to show when you hop to another theme park on the same day. If you're staying at a Walt Disney World hotel, theme park standard parking is complimentary, but you can upgrade to preferred parking for an average of $20 (good at all four parks).

55.
Find Annual Passholder Perks

If you are visiting Walt Disney World for ten days or more within a twelve-month span, you will break even on the cost of an Annual Pass and receive Annual Passholder perks such as free parking at theme parks, and discounts on food, merchandise, backstage tours, special events, sports, and recreation. All of those perks apply over the course of the pass's one-year time frame, no matter how many times you visit. Only one person in your group needs to be an Annual Passholder for the dining and merchandise discounts and the free parking perks to apply, as long as that person is in attendance at the time of use.

56.
Make Tap Water Palatable

Unless you live in an area with a high limestone concentration, your water at home probably doesn't taste like Florida water. The peninsula's limestone base means a great deal of calcium and magnesium leach into the ground water, and that "hard water" flavor definitely comes through in the tap water. While it isn't a health issue, its sharp taste has a rather infamous reputation with visitors. With that in mind, bring along portable flavoring packets, such as Crystal Light, sports-drink powder, or those drops your teens put into their water bottles that come in colors never found in nature. Multipacket boxes are available at most dollar stores, Walmart, or any of Orlando's grocery stores, and they help mask the unusual taste.

57.
Inexpensive Glow Toys

As the sun begins to set over the theme parks, the carts selling light-up novelties come out in full force, and their entire focus is on tempting you and your youngsters to purchase a glow toy from their wide selection of wands, spinners, necklaces, lanyards, and character-themed items. If you have the budget for it (up to $30!), there are some truly attractive options. If you prefer to put your money toward something else, pick up glow sticks, glow wands, and light-up necklaces at your local dollar store or craft shop. Watch for Christmas bulb necklaces during the holiday season, which are nearly identical to those sold at Walt Disney World, but at half the price.

58.
Save for Collectibles

Orlando is all about having fun, letting go, being wacky, and even splurging on some fanciful item you will never, ever wear once you leave Disney property. It's a vacation; it's meant to be something special and out of the ordinary. But you're looking to save money too. By purchasing items such as rain ponchos, water bottles, and glow sticks at a discount or dollar store, you'll have those few extra dollars to put toward a Goofy hat or an "I'm with Grumpy" T-shirt. Get even more bang for your buck by purchasing merchandise themed for festivals, special events, or land or attraction openings, especially if it includes a date. These items are highly collectible, and even more so when left in the original, unopened packaging.

59.
Never Pay for Water

The only time you should purchase bottled water in the theme parks or water parks is during the heat of summer when you've forgotten your reusable water bottle and all the water mains are broken (meaning, never). All counter-service restaurants will provide a small cup of water, with or without ice, upon request, even if you haven't purchased a meal, food item, or other drink. Simply ask the cashier for water or ice water, and he'll provide you with a receipt you can take to the food pick-up counter. Hand it to the Cast Member assembling food and drink trays, and she'll cheerfully provide you with the aforementioned hydration. During really hot periods, ice water dispensers will be available at the parks, resorts, and Disney Springs.

60.
Make Use of Hydration Stations

Water bottle filling stations (or Hydration Stations) are located in all four theme parks (plus Disney Springs and some hotels). New ones keep popping up, but here's where you can find some of them in the parks:

- **Hollywood Studios**—Near the Standby queue for Slinky Dog Dash, inside the exit for Millennium Falcon: Smugglers Run, near the restrooms in Star Wars: Galaxy's Edge, and by the Skyliner station (outside the park).
- **Animal Kingdom**—In the Standby queues for Avatar Flight of Passage and Na'vi River Journey.
- **EPCOT**—At EPCOT Experience, near Journey of Water, Inspired by Moana, and the Odyssey Events Pavilion.
- **Magic Kingdom**—Inside Cosmic Ray's Starlight Café, Pinocchio Village Haus, and outside the TRON Lightcycle/Run restrooms.

61.
Pressed Pennies

Disney's least expensive souvenir is a pressed penny, with over five hundred designs available throughout Walt Disney World. Luckily, you won't have to haul a heavy bag of coins because the machines will provide the pennies. You will, however, need one-dollar bills (a credit card is accepted if you want to purchase all the designs at a machine).

62.
Get the "Princess Look" for Less

Princesses love their pampering, and no place does it better than Bibbidi Bobbidi Boutique at Disney Springs and inside Cinderella Castle at Magic Kingdom. With packages starting at $70 and running well past $450, this hair, nails, makeup, and costume salon for ages three to twelve can break many guests' budget. Instead, pay a visit to Walmart or Target for princess-wear ($15–$35); arrange your child's hair into a tight bun, high on the head (hint: use lots of hair gel and bobby pins, and apply hairspray liberally); add a play tiara ($2–$12); dip into your makeup kit and nail polish; and voilà! A perfect princess for a fraction of the cost. Not sure how to do the "princess" bun? Search for "ballet bun tutorial" on YouTube. If you're just looking for a bit of sparkle, princes and princesses of all ages can stop at Sir Mickey's in Fantasyland and ask for a free pixie dusting.

Score Free Stuff at Disney

Along with Mickey stickers and the ever-popular Kidcot Fun Stops throughout World Showcase in EPCOT, where kids receive a craft item they can decorate in each country, there are lots of little freebies to watch for at the parks, resorts, and Disney Springs.

63. The best free item you can get in each of the four Disney parks are the "celebration" buttons found at Guest Services (City Hall at Magic Kingdom). These pin-on buttons highlight special dates such as anniversaries, birthdays, first visits, and the catch-all "I'm Celebrating." Why are they the best? Because they lead to lots of well-wishes from Cast Members, and they occasionally result in another freebie such as a cupcake or a front-row seat on Soarin' Around the World.

64. When Magic Kingdom is busy, you'll often see a Cast Member from the Main Street Confectionery standing outside with a tray of small samples, such as cookies, candy, sweet drinks, ice cream, or cotton candy, for a magical treat as you start your walk down Main Street. If there's nobody outside when you pass by, pop into the shop and see if they're offering samples inside.

65. Sample Coca-Cola beverages from around the world at Club Cool in World Celebration at EPCOT. Self-serve dispensers allow guests to try unusual sodas from eight countries, including oddities such as Bon Bon Anglais from Madagascar, Country Club Merengue from Dominican Republic, Minute Maid Joy Apple Lychee from Korea, Royal Wattamelon from the Philippines, Smart Sour Plum from China, Sprite Cucumber from Russia, and Viva Raspberry from Moldova. The anti-favorite Beverly from Italy continues to delight returning visitors pranking unsuspecting newbies. The only limit on how many you can try is your tolerance level for sweet beverages (not you, bitter Beverly).

66. Disney Springs has some of the best restaurants on-site, but whether you dine there and are too full for more than a small treat for dessert, or if you're just wandering around and a chocolate craving takes hold, Ghirardelli Soda Fountain and Chocolate Shop hands out free chocolate squares. They're just a one- or two-bite square, perfect for keeping your sweet tooth at bay.

67. Each of the Disney Deluxe and Moderate resorts offers evening campfires, weather and seasonal conditions permitting, with activities, sing-alongs, possibly a character or two, and that quintessential campfire family favorite: marshmallow roasting. All Disney resort guests can join in, and it's even more fun when you make a night of it by staying out for another freebie, Movies Under the Stars.

68. Whether or not you attend the campfire program, Movies Under the Stars is such a wonderful way to end your day that even the Value resorts offer them. All movies are family-friendly Disney and Pixar films, and it's okay to hop to a resort other than your own if it's showing one of your favorites, or if your own resort's movie is one you've already seen.

Disney Pins: Real or Fake?

When purchasing trading pins on eBay, check a few key authenticity markers. Official pins have a Mickey head logo with a banner across it that reads "Pin Trading" and a date on the back of the pin, plus "© Disney." They feature a small nub on one or both sides of the stick pin, and every element is extremely precise. Incorrect character colors, pockmarks in the paint, rough edges, spelling errors, a dull finish, and imprecise lines are hallmarks of fakes or "scrappers." If it's a layered pin, has hinges, or has moving elements, it's probably real. Sold in bulk? Fake. But don't worry, grownups—Disney Cast Members will always trade pins with kids (even if the pins are fake).

69.
Check Out Fort Wilderness Golf Cart Parades

The annual Mickey's Not-So-Scary Halloween Party and Mickey's Very Merry Christmas Party are beloved seasonal additions, but they can also add over $500 to your vacation expenses for a family of four. If something a bit less taxing on the wallet is in order, you won't be left out. Head over to Fort Wilderness Resort and Campground between October 30 and December 24 for the quirkiest, most imaginative guest-created holiday parades you'll ever see. Campers decorate their golf carts with elaborate themes, such as the *Millennium Falcon*, Haunted Mansion, or Santa's sleigh; Disney characters are on hand; and there are prizes for the best-decorated carts. Date and time are subject to change, so phone Fort Wilderness Guest Services at 407-824-2900 for current information.

70.
Target RedCard Discount

When is $950 worth a thousand dollars? When it's on Disney Gift Cards purchased with your Target RedCard. Each time you use your Target RedCard to purchase a Disney Gift Card you receive 5 percent off the price, and the cards can be used to pay for park admission, resort rooms, shopping, and dining all across Walt Disney World (with a few exceptions, such as some food and gift kiosks). The discount can be applied to all Disney Gift Cards purchased in-store or online, and they are a good way to help control the budget if you're trying to avoid impulse buying or limit children's spending on souvenirs. Use the $50 savings on another card, or as "mad money" for a family splurge in the parks.

71.

Take a Fort Wilderness Rest Day

Fort Wilderness has so much going on you can easily make it a full day's adventure. Purchase park admission for one less day than you have available and enjoy the free or inexpensive activities at Mickey's campground. Take to the waterways in a canoe, kayak, or boat; try your hand at archery; tour the barns where Magic Kingdom's horses live; stroll the walking trails; or rent bikes or a surrey bike. For a few dollars more, go horseback riding or take a wagon or sleigh ride. Treat children to a pony ride or time at the playground, then end your day with the free Chip 'n' Dale's Campfire Sing-A-Long. Grand finale? Watch the Electrical Water Pageant from the shores of Bay Lake.

72.

Avoid Discount-Ticket Scammers

You've arrived in Orlando for an unplanned one- or two-day visit, and the booths dotting the tourist areas with signs for "Discounted Disney Tickets," or the discounted tickets on eBay or Craigslist, hold tremendous appeal. These are partially used, nontransferable tickets purchased by previous Orlando tourists, and you're in for a massive disappointment once you reach Disney's front-gate biometric scanners. Even if they *have* any days left on them, your finger-scan won't match, nor will Disney refund your money, and you'll be left holding worthless tickets. Instead, check out www.mousesavers.com's list of authorized Walt Disney World ticket sellers or try local authorized ticket outlet Orlando Attractions, www.orlandoattractions.com. You'll pay more than you would with a scammer, but you'll also get through the front gates.

73.
Save at Disney's Character Warehouse

Authentic Disney merchandise for up to 50 percent off? Yes, please! Everyone likes to open gifts with a little "Disney" inside, but on-site prices can be hard on tight budgets. Save a few bucks with a trip to Disney's Character Warehouse in the Orlando Vineland Premium Outlets shopping center, just three miles from Walt Disney World. Another big bonus? Much of the merchandise is last-season or discontinued, so you might find that item you wish you'd bought during your last Disney vacation. Can't find what you want? There is a second location at Orlando International Premium Outlets.

74.
Use Your Costco Member Discounts

That Costco membership you use to purchase forty rolls of toilet paper, massive bags of tortilla chips, and meat by the ton can come in handy for your Disney vacation too. Most Costco stores carry gift cards for discounts on Disney theme park tickets, or percentage-off cards for Disney resort rooms. For online discounts, visit www.costcotravel.com, and click on "Theme Parks & Specialty" to go straight to Walt Disney World for discounts specific to Disney and the surrounding area. Some package deals include extras, such as room upgrades or kids-eat-free discounts. Or click on "Hotels" and input your details if you don't need add-ons such as theme park tickets or a rental car. Be sure to compare with other discount sites to find the best savings.

75.
Find Passholder Snack Discounts

One of the big benefits of being an Annual Passholder is the discount you'll receive at many dining locations, but what if you just want a small snack? You're in luck. Annual Passholders receive a 10, 15, or 20 percent discount on food and nonalcoholic beverages at Erin McKenna's Bakery NYC; Häagen-Dazs Kiosk; Joffrey's Coffee & Tea Company; Joffrey's Handcrafted Smoothies; Sprinkles; Vivoli il Gelato; and Wetzel's Pretzels Kiosk, all at Disney Springs, plus Beaches & Cream Soda Shop at Disney's Beach Club Resort. You can also purchase snacks and drinks at select merchandise locations and receive the discount. Always ask if the Annual Passholder discount applies.

76.
Pro Alert: Use Credit Card Points

Investigate your existing credit card or hotel loyalty program for any perks you can use or points you can apply toward your vacation expenses. If you take out a new credit card for its introductory points, make certain you can reach their bonus points requirements and be sure they waive the first year's fee. Purchasing your flights or park tickets on your new credit card will start you on the right track toward reaching any spending requirements, which often must be met within thirty days of activating your card. Then, apply the bonus points to pay down your balance, or use them to pay for other vacation expenses. Place a reminder in your calendar to cancel the card and avoid paying the second year's annual fee.

77.
Eat at Themed Restaurants for Less

Your budget is tight, but you'd still like to see the wonderfully themed Be Our Guest Restaurant, with its ballroom, West Wing, and Rose Gallery rooms, which can only be toured by guests with a dining reservation. The prix fixe dinner costs more than $100 for two adults or over $200 for a family of four, which isn't exactly wallet-friendly. Instead, make an off-peak lunch reservation and enjoy the dramatic elements in each room without a hefty bill. It's okay if you just order dessert or appetizers at Be Our Guest, or at any of Disney's non-buffet or no-characters restaurants. Jungle Navigation Co. LTD Skipper Canteen in Magic Kingdom, Black Spire Outpost's Docking Bay 7 in Hollywood Studios, Space 220 Lounge in EPCOT, Rainforest Cafe at Animal Kingdom and Disney Springs, and T-REX at Disney Springs have the best themed environments.

78.
Do Deluxe Resorts on a Budget

Disney's Deluxe-level resorts are spectacular, from their themes to their special amenities, and your dream is to experience one or more of them in your lifetime. Your budget, however, says otherwise. Don't despair. While it may take a bit more saving, there is a solution: Book the majority of your stay at a Value resort, and book your final night at a Deluxe. Save money by purchasing one less day on your park pass than you otherwise would, and spend the day before your departure enjoying the resort. Stay off-site for the first part of your vacation for added savings and apply the difference to your Deluxe room.

Discover Cheaper Versions of
Expensive Experiences

You won't have the same five-star dining experience anywhere on Disney property that you'll get at the exclusive Victoria & Albert's Restaurant, or the feel of a Starlight Safari tour on the savanna at Animal Kingdom Lodge, but if your goal is to save money while still getting the flavor of an experience and making memories with your loved ones, there are some good alternatives to the expensive options.

79. **Bibbidi Bobbidi Boutique is a dream experience for many little girls, but it can be a nightmare on the wallet.** It's easy to create the look yourself for far less (see hack #62: "Get the 'Princess Look' for Less" earlier in this chapter). Added bonus? Kids under age three can get the regal at-home treatment too. Hook up with the 2 p.m. Princess Parade at Disney Springs and "their majesty" will get a free ride on the carousel. All "royalty" is allowed to participate, even if they didn't get their makeovers at Bibbidi Bobbidi Boutique.

80. **Magic Kingdom, EPCOT, and Hollywood Studios offer paid-for dessert parties during their nighttime shows,** with a selection of mini sweet treats, fruits, savories, and drinks in a private viewing area. As beautiful as the desserts are and as convenient as it is to avoid looking for the perfect viewing area (of which there are many, for free), they will set a family of four back by $300 or more, depending on ages of children. The less expensive option involves a visit to Main Street Bakery in Magic Kingdom, Les Halles Boulangerie-Patisserie in EPCOT, or The Trolley Car Café in Hollywood Studios. You can even add the adult libation of your choice as a grand finale to a magical day.

81. Jellyrolls has a cover charge, and you're going to want drinks as well. Instead, check out the free live music at Disney Springs, and bring your own booze. Sit down at The Front Porch at House of Blues or Raglan Road's indoor or outdoor bar, if you don't mind springing for a drink. Disney's BoardWalk has fewer entertainers, but they're worth seeing if you're also visiting for Movies Under the Stars at BoardWalk or the Yacht and Beach Club resorts.

82. Other inexpensive options for on-site guests are viewing the Magic Kingdom fireworks from the Grand Floridian Resort's ferry dock (where you may hear the fireworks' soundtrack from Narcoosee's and you'll see each burst reflected on Seven Seas Lagoon) rather than booking a fireworks cruise, and casting a line in at the Fishin' Hole at Ol' Man Island at Port Orleans Resort–Riverside (instead of paying for a catch-and-release guided fishing tour).

Get Unlimited Photos with Memory Maker

Want unlimited PhotoPass in-park photos, dining photos, still and animated Magic Shots, and on-ride photos and videos? Purchase Memory Maker online (four days or more before arrival, for the discounted price), and go wild! Ride photos and video will automatically be added to your account if your MagicBand, park ticket, or PhotoPass card is linked to your My Disney Experience account. Memory Maker is also a paid-for add-on for Annual Passes, and only one person needs an Annual Pass to receive the perk, as long as everyone is linked via "Family & Friends" on your My Disney Experience app. Free digital downloads of select Disney PhotoPass attraction photos taken in the parks are also included on each day you purchase Disney Genie+.

83.
Evaluate Discounts Carefully

Not all discounts are created equal. Paying for a resort room or park tickets using Disney Gift Cards at the RedCard 5 percent discount, for example, may not be cheaper than booking the same room or tickets through a non-Disney vendor. When a better room or ticket discount is available, use your Disney Gift Cards on meals or merchandise that would otherwise have no discount. For longer stays, purchasing an Annual Pass for one person may prove a big savings over buying a park pass when factoring in food and merchandise discounts, and free parking. That "free" Disney Dining Plan may cost more as a package than you'd pay for a discounted room and the amount of food you would normally eat.

84.
Pro Alert: Discounts in Unexpected Places

Before purchasing park passes, hotels, flights, or a rental car, you're going to do a lot of research to ensure you get the best deal possible. While large aggregators such as Expedia, Skyscanner, Travelocity, and KAYAK are obvious sites for price comparisons, there are a few less-obvious options worth exploring. Ask your employer if they offer member discounts through www.ticketsatwork.com. American Automobile Association (AAA) members receive Walt Disney World ticket discounts, either online at AAA Travel or by visiting your local AAA office. TripAdvisor often runs special discount deals for Orlando hotels on www.tripadvisor.com, and Disney-specific online sites with reliable reputations, such as www.mousesavers.com and authorized Disney ticket seller www .undercovertourist.com, feature theme park tickets and resort or rental car discounts.

85.
Let Your Travel Agent Find a Discount

Travel agents are a great resource (even for Walt Disney World pros). Your travel agent can make dining and Genie+ reservations, but they also get a heads up from Disney about upcoming discount offers, so they'll be the one getting up at an ungodly hour and waiting on hold when Disney releases the best discount codes. Although these discounts are available to the public, codes with the biggest savings are limited, and will be gone if you're not among the first to request them. Travel agents can also add discounts to existing reservations, which you can't always do if you book on your own. Best of all, there are no fees to use their services.

86.
Picnic in the Parks

Dining in the on-site restaurants is one of the great joys of a Disney vacation, but even purchasing quick-service meals two or three times a day can be hard on the wallet. Disney does allow guests to bring certain foods into the parks, and an impromptu picnic can be just as enjoyable when eaten in scenic surroundings. Sandwiches and other foods that do not need heating are allowed; as are snacks, chips, raw vegetables, and wrapped, prepared foods. Just be sure the items you bring don't need refrigeration. Alcohol is not allowed, and glass containers other than baby food jars are also forbidden. You can bring a small cooler, but remember, you'll be lugging it around all day or paying to store it in a locker.

87.
Grab Disney Springs Hotels Special Offers

Guests who want the convenience of staying on Disney property without the Disney resort prices will quickly become familiar with the Hotel Plaza Boulevard hotels, which are on-site but not owned by Disney. Each advertises special offers on their individual websites, including loyalty-program specials, AAA discounts, and "additional nights free" deals. While you're doing your comparison shopping for a budget-friendly bargain, don't overlook the offers featured on www.disneyspringshotels.com/special-offers. Each of the Hotel Plaza resorts lists unique specials, such as "kids eat free," gift card incentives, and promotional rates on suites, which you may not find on their websites. Bear in mind, these special offers tend to be package deals, so compare the value of any added benefits against room-only prices.

88.
Find Water Park Fun for Less

You have seven full days at Walt Disney World and you want to visit a water park, but a seven-day Park Hopper Plus ticket stretches the budget. It's within reach, if you're creative with your ticket options. For six park days and one water park day, the best savings comes from purchasing a six-day Base Ticket and a separate single-day Water Park Ticket. If you'll visit theme parks on just five of your seven days, the five-day Park Hopper Plus ticket provides the best value. If you'd like two water park days and maximum flexibility, the six-day or seven-day Base Ticket with Park Hopper Plus are both a better value than a five-day Base Ticket with two separate Water Park Tickets.

89.
Don't Miss the PhotoPass Service Studio

Annual Passholders and guests using Memory Maker shouldn't miss out on the most elaborate PhotoPass opportunity in all of Walt Disney World. When you've exhausted your options in the parks, head to Disney Springs for the PhotoPass Service Studio and its selection of backgrounds. Choose the background or "virtual backdrop" you love the most, add a prop if you're so inclined, stand in front of the green screen, and snap! A photo worthy of this year's holiday cards. The photos are added to your My Disney Experience account with the purchase of Memory Maker, but anyone can use the service without obligation and purchase photos individually. Be sure to ask for two or three backdrops.

Customize Disney Gift Cards

Whether you're giving a Disney Gift Card as a gift, or you're just trying to keep the kids' souvenir spending to a dull roar during your Walt Disney World vacation, make each card special for the receiver by visiting www.shopdisney.com, and selecting from more than seventy themed cards. Scroll to the bottom of the page, then click "Gift Cards." Disney Gift Cards never expire. You can add more money to each, or consolidate any remaining balances onto one account. Be sure to photograph the back of each card so they can be canceled and replaced if any of them get lost.

90.
Have a Happy Hour at Disney Springs

Watching your wallet doesn't mean you can't enjoy superb food and creative cocktails. Disney Springs has become the go-to spot for happy hour and late-night dining menus, with some restaurants, such as Jock Lindsey's Hangar Bar, offering dishes large enough for two at prices you'd expect for one. STK Orlando is hard to beat for inexpensive social-hour bites, brews, wine, and select cocktails. Just looking for a drink? The Front Porch at House of Blues offers exceptional prices and free live music, while Terralina Crafted Italian features drink specials on the patio overlooking the lake. Craft beer drinker? Head to happy hour at Planet Hollywood's Stargazers Bar. Feel like wandering? Disney Springs is a "licensed area," and most locations will give you a to-go cup.

91.
Clear Flight Search Cookies

You've checked all the flight prices for your Orlando trip, you've narrowed it down to a few possibilities, but you're not quite ready to hit "Pay" yet. When the time comes, pause a moment before you log on to the booking site again or that great price you found may be "gone." Because airline booking sites use cookies to track visitation, the price you see upon returning may be higher. Clear your computer's cache before searching a second time. You'll look like a new customer without an established interest, and that price you liked won't be artificially inflated because the booking engine "saw" your previous activity. Additionally, comparison shopping from a different IP address sometimes results in lower prices.

92.
Take Advantage of 24-Hour Cancellations

Some airlines allow you to hold a ticket for free or for a nominal fee from one day up to one week, which will allow time to see if fares go down before purchasing. Even when you buy a ticket, you always have 24 hours to cancel for free if the fares change.

93.
Get a Military Memory Maker

Although Memory Maker, the unlimited PhotoPass digital photo add-on, is available to anyone, a special Military Memory Maker is offered at a deeply discounted price for active and retired military guests. But you won't find it online. There are only two ways it can be purchased: in person at Guest Services or through Disney's on-site ticket agents. Stop at any Guest Services or theme park ticketing window, show the Cast Member your military identification, and ask for the discounted Memory Maker. A military member's spouse may also purchase the discounted service by presenting an active military identification. Your Memory Maker will become active immediately. Easiest way to do it? Purchase Memory Maker when you activate your military-discount theme park tickets.

94.
Upgrade to an Annual Pass

You're at Walt Disney World and you realize that this "once in a lifetime" trip is really just the first of many. If you're planning your next visit before the current one has ended, you have at least one full day left on your current tickets, fewer than fourteen days have elapsed since you first used them, and your next trip will be within twelve months of the date of first use, you can upgrade your current passes to Annual Passes and reap all the benefits. Ideally you will have purchased your original ticket at a discounted price, because the non-discounted value of your park pass will be applied to the cost of the Annual Pass when you upgrade in person at any Guest Services.

95.
Disney Visa Card Membership

Although other credit cards offer bigger cash-back incentives, there are some perks you'll only get with a Disney Rewards Visa Card, and that makes it worth considering. Have a Star Wars fanatic in your group? Along with a host of dining, shopping, spa service, and recreation discounts, cardmembers enjoy private access to select Star Wars characters and other Disney characters, with free photos to commemorate their encounters. Exclusive merchandise, discounts, cardmember events, expanded booking dates for the free Disney Dining Plan, no annual fee, and a tidy sign-up bonus (with required minimum use) add to the value, even if you only use the card during your vacation and use other cards for everyday purchases. You can even choose from ten different Disney-themed designs.

96.
Reimburse Yourself for Airline Tickets

Disney Visa Premier cardmembers can use their Disney Rewards Dollars to reimburse themselves for airline tickets bought with their card. Just purchase tickets directly with the airline, travel agent, or travel website, and pay yourself back within sixty days by redeeming Disney Dollars for a statement credit. Don't have enough Disney Dollars to cover the entire ticket price? You can still apply a lower amount for credit toward the cost.

CHAPTER 3

PLANES, TRAMS, AND AUTOMOBILES

97.
Fly in the Morning

The quickest way for out-of-state visitors to reach Orlando is usually by airplane. But what if you're a passenger who spends the whole ride gripping the armrests, dreading fearful flyers' number one trigger, turbulence? If the mantra "turbulence isn't dangerous" doesn't soothe your jangled nerves, your seat and time of day might. While a smooth flight is always likely, booking a morning departure may help. Florida's afternoon thunderstorms make midday flying in summertime more prone to turbulence before landing and after takeoff, and air currents are less riled early in the day. Book the second morning flight rather than the first, so that any turbulent areas are known to the pilots. They can often route around them. Seats over the wings experience less movement too.

98.
Snap an Airport Parking Photo

The excitement of being on your way to Walt Disney World, and the unfamiliar routine of getting to the airport and navigating through security, can take up a lot of mental energy. By the time you've taken your flight, enjoyed a fantastic vacation, and returned to your home airport, there is an excellent chance you will have forgotten where you parked. Take a page out of the Disney parking lot playbook and snap a photo of your parking space row and number on your cell phone. You'll be glad you have it when you get back. Before handing them over, take a photo of your suitcases that will travel as checked luggage. If they are misplaced, you can show the airport agent exactly what they look like.

99.
Newbie Alert: You're Not Going to Orlando

You've arrived at Orlando International Airport (MCO), you've picked up your rental car, and now it's time to hit the highway for your vacation with Mickey Mouse. But wait. Don't follow the airport signs to Orlando. Walt Disney World is in Lake Buena Vista, twenty miles south of downtown Orlando. Instead, choose one of two options: Take the south exit to State Road 417, pick up World Center Drive (Exit 6) to reach the heart of Walt Disney World, then follow resort signs (take SR 417 to West Osceola Parkway at Exit 6 for Highway 192 resorts); or take the north exit to State Road 528 (Beachline Expressway West), merge onto Interstate 4, and follow signs to off-site resort locations or Disney Springs. Each route includes tolls.

100.
Fly the "Hidden" Airline

Low-cost carrier Allegiant Air flies nonstop to Orlando Sanford International Airport (SFB) from seventy-one cities across the Northeast, Midwest, Southeast, and Southwest, but they do not show up on aggregator searches for flights. Check www .allegiantair.com for their route map and special deals, which are often cheaper than other airlines'. Be sure to factor in luggage fees and other add-ons, such as in-flight snacks and drinks, as well as the cost of car rental and highway tolls over a taxi, Uber, or Lyft from Orlando International Airport (MCO). Sanford is forty-seven miles northwest of Walt Disney World, making a rental car necessary.

101.
Scope Out Inexpensive Gas

Unlike literally everything else you will purchase at Walt Disney World, gas at the Speedway stations on Walt Disney World property is often less expensive than filling up at off-site gas stations, especially those within a mile or two of Disney. Look for locations on the corner of World Drive and Car Care Drive near Disney's Polynesian Village and Grand Floridian Resorts; on Buena Vista Drive across from Disney Springs; and on the corner of East Buena Vista Drive and EPCOT Resorts Boulevard in front of the Board-Walk Inn. Each has a convenience store with refreshments if you need a quick snack or drink as you drive between parks.

102.
Get "OK Maps"

You may want to venture off Disney property, and for that you'll need a map to help you find your way around. Even if you won't leave Disney property, remember, Walt Disney World is forty square miles (nearly the size of Boston!), and while signage is good, roads can still be confusing. Download the Google Maps app to your cell phone, iPad, or tablet, pull up Lake Buena Vista, zoom in to the area you want to save, tap the search bar, type "OK Maps" (without quotation marks), then click "Search." You'll be able to see the map even when you're offline. For voice commands, say "O" and then "K," with a few seconds' pause between the two. Once the map shows as cached, you're all set!

103.
Keep Kids Happy with a DIY In-Flight Movie

No movie on your flight? Load your tablet with your or your children's favorite movie or show, slip it into a gallon-sized Ziploc, and secure it to the closed tray table in front of you using the tray's lock mechanism. For a sturdy holder when driving, purchase a clear, zippered pencil pouch with pre-made holes (the kind you snap into a three-ring binder), making sure it's big enough to hold your tablet. Thread a long strip of ribbon through each of the two end holes, tying the ribbon tight to the pencil holder. Insert the tablet into the pouch so the screen shows through the plastic, tie the pouch to the car's headrest stand, and connect long-cord headphones. Instant hands-free viewing, with easy zipper access.

104.
Hack a Burger-and-Fries Caddy

When your drive to Orlando is long enough to require a meal, keep the car seats free from spills by purchasing an inexpensive, plastic shower caddy—the kind with a handle in the middle and a section on either side—not only for storing items such as kid's toys, crayons, and other small items, but also as a handy holder at mealtimes. Make sure the sections on each side of the handle are wide enough to hold a can or to-go cup if you don't have enough cup holders in the car. The sections will be just the right size for keeping a burger and fries upright too.

105.
Beat the Heat with a Scald-Free Steering Wheel

When visiting Orlando between April and October, it's a given you'll need a foldable sunshade to insert between the dashboard and the front window to keep the interior of your car from becoming an inferno. If you don't have one, all is not lost. Once you're parked, but before you switch off the engine, turn the steering wheel as far as possible so that the top is pointed toward the driver's seat. When it returns to its correct position it won't be as blistering hot as it would be otherwise, and the driver won't suffer scalded hands. Then, spend a minute with the air conditioner on full blast and the car doors or windows open. The air will help blow the interior heat out quickly.

106.
Save on Baggage Fees

Make the most of the free "personal item" on low-cost carriers by giving each child a full-sized bag that meets the airline's dimension restrictions. Choose mix-and-match clothing, leave everything that isn't essential at home, and wear bulkier shoes and clothing while you're in transit. Short vacations may not require additional luggage, while longer vacations may need one checked bag. Be sure to put your phone, medications, and any other items you may need in a smaller bag inside the larger bag in case the overhead bins are full and the flight attendants have to check your carry-on bag at the last minute. You can remove the smaller bag quickly and still have necessities on hand during the flight.

107.
Newbie Alert:
Remember Where You Parked

You're in the happiest place on Earth and also in one of the largest parking lots on Earth. With a full day's excitement in store, you won't remember your Simba from your Jafar by nightfall, and actual row numbers will be a mental blur by the time you stagger back to your car. Avoid looking like a sad, disoriented rookie by taking a photo of your row number after you've parked your car, either with your cell phone or your digital camera. You'll be glad for the quick reminder in a sea of rental cars that all look the same in the dark. There is also a Car Locator feature in the My Disney Experience app, but you do have to remember to enter your car's location. Worst case? Locate a parking attendant Cast Member and tell them what time you arrived. They can point you toward the correct few rows.

108.
Resort-to-Resort Transportation

You cannot take a bus from one Disney resort to another, so if you are not using your own car or a rental and you're planning on having a meal at a resort without a boat or monorail connection, you'll have to change buses at the Transportation and Ticket Center, at a theme park, or at Disney Springs. The process can take sixty to ninety minutes, depending on your location. If time is of the essence, Mears Transportation or a Minnie Van Connected by Lyft is your best choice. Minnie Van service has a $22 base price, plus a per-mile charge, so a Mears luxury sedan, SUV, or van may be cheaper. Download the Mears Taxi app, or go to www.mearstransportation.com, enter your location and your destination, and you'll get an estimate of the cost.

Disney Without a Car

Overnight hotel self-parking and standard parking at all four theme parks is complimentary for Walt Disney World Resort hotel guests; however, you can avoid renting a car if you know you'll be staying on Disney property only, and take advantage of the on-site transportation options via bus, boat, skyliner, and monorail.

109. **All guests are allowed to use Disney's buses and monorail for free, and often they are the right choice.** The monorail is ideal for traveling to Magic Kingdom and EPCOT when staying at a Magic Kingdom resort (Polynesian Village, Contemporary, or Grand Floridian), and the bus is nearly always a great choice, with a few notable exceptions.

110. **If time is of the essence due to a Genie+ ride time or dining reservation and you're traveling to Magic Kingdom from a resort or location that isn't on the monorail system, skip the long bus ride** (or the tedious transitions from the parking lot if you're driving), and call for a Minnie Van. It will cost you, but you'll be dropped off right at the front of the park without the need to pass through the Transportation and Ticket Center and transfer to a boat or the monorail.

111. **Heading to Fort Wilderness for some cowboy-style fun?** Driving or using the bus system will require you to park or exit the bus at Outpost Depot, at the front of Fort Wilderness, and make the twenty-five minute walk to Settlement Trading Post at the back of the campground, or transfer to a Fort Wilderness bus and endure several stops along the way.

A Minnie Van is your best choice, with a drop-off point at Tri-Circle-D Ranch, just a few minutes' stroll from Pioneer Hall.

112. Guests staying at the Polynesian Village Resort can walk to the Transportation and Ticket Center to pick up the monorail to EPCOT. It's quicker than making the circuit to Magic Kingdom and transferring to the EPCOT monorail.

113. Wilderness Lodge, Grand Floridian, Polynesian Village, and Fort Wilderness each have a direct service to Magic Kingdom via boat. Staying at the Contemporary Resort? You have the most convenient resort of all for a quick walk to Magic Kingdom.

114. The Yacht Club, Beach Club, BoardWalk, and the Swan and Dolphin Resorts have boat service to EPCOT and Hollywood Studios. With stops at each resort, the full circuit between EPCOT and Hollywood Studios takes roughly thirty minutes, which is approximately how long it would take if you walk. There is no bus between these resorts and Hollywood Studios or EPCOT.

115. Staying at Riviera Resort or Caribbean Beach Resort? Take the Skyliner gondola to EPCOT from Riviera, or to Hollywood Studios from Caribbean Beach.

116.
Steer Clear of Exploding Diapers

Every parent has experienced the dreaded "exploding diaper," a situation so foul no human being should be forced to endure it. But, as they say, "stuff happens," and sometimes it happens on an airplane. Carry a diaper, wipes, a disposable changing pad, a diaper pail liner, and a change of clothes in a large Ziploc bag, and stick it in the pocket on the back of the seat in front of you. Being able to pull it out quickly and have everything ready to go will keep you, your baby, and everyone around you happy if things get smelly. Tie the diaper up in the pail liner for disposal and use the Ziploc bag to carry messy clothes until they can be laundered.

117.
Take the Bus

Staying at a Walt Disney World resort has its benefits, but sometimes it just doesn't fit into the budget. International Drive, seven miles to the north, is among the most popular off-site hotel destinations, because it's walkable and is chock-full of minor attractions, restaurants, and shopping outlets. While many hotels provide a shuttle to Disney property, those that do not are within easy walking distance of the LYNX bus stops. Catch the Number 8 bus to the SeaWorld stop and transfer to the Number 350 bus (with its pick-up location directly across Sea Harbor Drive), which takes you to Disney property. From there, use Disney's free internal bus system, which can be slower but more cost-effective.

118.
Hop Aboard the Disney Springs Ferryboat

Guests staying at Old Key West, Port Orleans–Riverside and French Quarter, and Saratoga Springs Resorts have easy access to Disney Springs via ferryboat, but non-resort guests are welcome to use it too. Disney Springs requires a lot of walking, so when you're ready for time off your feet, but you don't want to sit through a movie or have a meal, catch the ferryboat for a free round-trip excursion. It's a relaxing one-hour journey that generates a welcome breeze on a hot day as it winds along Lake Buena Vista and the arteries connecting Disney Springs to the resorts. Piped-in music and the boat captain's banter keeps families amused, but couples will find it surprisingly romantic at sunset, especially through the more secluded canals.

Airport Transportation

Mears Connect Driven by Sunshine offers reliable and affordable transportation between all three terminals at Orlando International Airport (MCO) and Walt Disney World Resort, with standard and express shuttle services available 24/7 to your hotel (kids under age three ride free with standard service). Private airport transfers are also available. You can either reserve your ride in advance or "on-the-spot" at the Mears Connect reception areas on level 1 of Terminals B and C. Mears Connect Driven by Sunshine is fully wheelchair-accessible and ADA-compliant.

119.
Pro Alert: Disney's Back-Door Entries

Visitors staying at Highway 27 or Highway 192 accommodations can use one of two semi-secret entries into Walt Disney World property, saving time over entering at World Drive, especially when visiting Animal Kingdom, Animal Kingdom Lodge, or Blizzard Beach Water Park. During peak hours (9 a.m. until noon), take State Road 429 to Western Way, then turn right for Animal Kingdom or left for the other parks. The route is one mile further and it includes a toll, but it avoids the heavy traffic of the more popular routes, and that matters a lot when you have a morning dining reservation or Genie+ time. During nonpeak hours, come in on Sherberth Road off Highway 192, which becomes slow going when morning traffic builds up.

120.
EarPlanes for Sensitive Ears

Your vacation is just a few days away and you've caught a cold. You're on vacation and the constant changes from Orlando's outdoor heat to the attractions' intense air conditioning have led to sinus trouble. Maybe it's just allergy season and you're suffering. Whatever the cause, your ears are now stuffed up and your airplane flight to or from Walt Disney World is imminent. Pop into CVS, Walgreens, Walmart, or Target in Orlando (or locations in your hometown) and pick up a set of EarPlanes to avoid pain during takeoff and landing. These earplugs are specially designed inserts that help keep your eustachian tubes open during changes in cabin pressure, thereby lessening the discomfort. Amazon Prime members can order EarPlanes for same-day delivery. They even come in a smaller size for kids.

121.
Go with High-Tech Parking at Disney Springs

Technology is great, except when it isn't. Disney Springs has some of the most technologically advanced parking structures imaginable, with digital signs at their entries showing how many spaces are open on each floor, additional digital signs on each floor with the same information, and drop-down lights at each parking space that indicate when that space is empty or taken. When the outdoor signs indicate the structure is full during peak times in busy seasons, it probably is, but before you give up, drive through if cars are not backed up outside. The inside signs don't always agree with the outside signs. Additionally, drop-down indicators are not always correct. If the lot is not bumper-to-bumper, you may get lucky and find a space.

122.
Park on Level 2

Finding a parking spot on the first floor of a multilevel structure is usually a good thing. At Disney Springs, however, it's not that simple. Instead of looking for a parking place on the first floor, take the ramp up to the second floor and look there. If you've parked on Level 1, you can't just walk into Disney Springs. You'll have to go up to Level 2, where visitors are required to cross a pedestrian bridge that leads from Level 2 back down to the shops and restaurants via escalators or an elevator. For the pedestrian bridge in the parking structure across Buena Vista Drive, park on Level 3.

123.
Make Your Road Trip Playlist

Knowing your car is pointed toward Walt Disney World will make everyone happy…at least for the first hour of your drive. After that, cue the impatient cries of "Are we there yet?" either out loud from children or silently from adults. That's where your Disney road trip playlist comes in. Create a playlist of Disney tunes, themed with travel songs, soundtracks from the theme park attractions, or the hits from classic Disney movies, and inform fellow riders it will only start when you're within thirty minutes of the parks. Choose upbeat songs and you'll be driving under the "Where Dreams Come True" sign singing and dancing in your seats. No time to make a playlist? The Play Disney Parks app has a road trip list already assembled.

Pack a Pashmina

A soft, comfy pashmina is your best travel companion, and with dozens of designs, they're not just limited to women. Roll it up and use it as a pillow on the airplane or in the car. It can be an instant blanket in transit, a picnic tablecloth, or bathing suit cover-up. Wear it to combat air conditioning in restaurants, buses, or monorails, or use it as a stroller pad or shade. Tie the ends together and make a bag or an impromptu vest, or wear it as a scarf. There are countless uses for this lightweight, versatile accessory.

124.
Keep Your Car Tidy

You have to make a long drive to Disney, but you're determined to do it in a tidy car. Start by placing silicone cupcake liners into cup holders to prevent condensation from mucking up the bottom. Carabiners hooked to the front seat headrest posts keep a trash bag and activity packs handy without cluttering up seats or foot wells. Rimmed cookie sheets make great play tables for youngsters, providing a stable surface for coloring and activity books while keeping small toys from sliding onto the floor. Let each child decorate their own tray in advance to avoid squabbles over who owns each one. Stick a lint roller into the glove box to pick up bits and pieces from the seats when you arrive.

125.
Get Around During runDisney Events

You've just discovered you're visiting Walt Disney World during a runDisney event. While crowd levels in the parks only go from low to moderate, road closures can occur the night before—and day of—events, causing traffic to back up; and parking lots where the race starts or finishes can be partially closed for staging areas, so they fill up quickly. Use Disney's on-site transportation on race day to help avoid closed roads, but allow plenty of travel time if you have a Genie+ or breakfast reservation, especially at Magic Kingdom, as buses drop off at the Transportation and Ticket Center during the race, and guests must use the monorail. When driving during January's Marathon Weekend, expect road disruptions until 1 p.m. and plan accordingly.

126.
Find the Airport Lost and Found

You spent days checking and rechecking your packing list prior to your vacation and were certain nothing was forgotten, or, like most people, you rushed around tying up loose ends for a week before your trip and only threw stuff into your suitcase the day before your departure. Whatever the reason, you've just realized you forgot your phone charger. Maybe you didn't bother packing an umbrella, and it's hammering down like nobody's business. Now what? Stop in at the Lost and Found when you arrive at the airport. Items that have gone unclaimed for more than ninety days are fair game, and if you ask nicely, you may avoid having to make a purchase. Orlando International's Lost and Found is located on Level 3, Side B.

127.
Lightning Lane Entrances

Some Lightning Lane entrances are offered through Genie+; others can be purchased individually. You can buy either or both options, but all Lightning Lane entrances are subject to availability, and are subject to change or closure without notice. It's a good idea to check the daily calendar in the My Disney Experience app or online for the dates of your visit to find out about scheduled refurbishments and closures. Lightning Lanes are available at the following attractions:

- **Animal Kingdom:** Festival of the Lion King, Expedition Everest–Legend of the Forbidden Mountain, Feathered Friends in Flight!, Finding Nemo: The Big Blue… and Beyond!, It's Tough to be a Bug!, Kali River Rapids, Kilimanjaro Safaris, Meet Favorite Disney Pals at Adventurers Outpost, Na'vi River Journey, and The Animation Experience at Conservation Station. Lightning Lane individual purchase: Avatar Flight of Passage.

- **EPCOT:** Disney and Pixar Short Film Festival, Frozen Ever After, Journey Into Imagination with Figment, Living with the Land, Mission: SPACE, Remy's Ratatouille Adventure, Soarin' Around the World, Spaceship Earth, Test Track, The Seas with Nemo & Friends, and Turtle Talk with Crush. Lightning Lane individual purchase: Guardians of the Galaxy: Cosmic Rewind.
- **Hollywood Studios:** Alien Swirling Saucers, Beauty and the Beast–Live on Stage, Disney Junior Play & Dance!, For the First Time in Forever: A Frozen Sing-Along Celebration, Indiana Jones Epic Stunt Spectacular!, Meet Olaf at Celebrity Spotlight, Mickey & Minnie's Runaway Railway, Millennium Falcon: Smugglers Run, Muppet*Vision 3D, Rock 'n' Roller Coaster Starring Aerosmith, Slinky Dog Dash, Star Tours–The Adventures Continue, The Twilight Zone Tower of Terror, and Toy Story Mania. Lightning Lane individual purchase: Star Wars: Rise of the Resistance.
- **Magic Kingdom:** Big Thunder Mountain Railroad, Buzz Lightyear's Space Ranger Spin, Disney Festival of Fantasy Parade, Dumbo the Flying Elephant, Enchanted Tales with Belle, Haunted Mansion, "it's a small world," Jungle Cruise, Mad Tea Party, Mickey's PhilharMagic, Monsters Inc. Laugh Floor, Peter Pan's Flight, Pirates of the Caribbean, Space Mountain, The Barnstormer, The Magic Carpets of Aladdin, The Many Adventures of Winnie the Pooh, Tomorrowland Speedway, Under the Sea–Journey of the Little Mermaid, and Meet Ariel at Her Grotto. Plus, meet and greets with Cinderella, Mickey, and Princess Tiana. Lightning Lane individual purchase: Seven Dwarfs Mine Train and TRON Lightcycle/Run.

128.
Prioritize Your Magic Kingdom Genie+ Attractions

In order of difficulty to obtain (or for ages six and under, in brackets): Space Mountain; Tiana's Bayou Adventure; Big Thunder Mountain Railroad; Jungle Cruise; Buzz Lightyear's Space Ranger Spin; Enchanted Tales with Belle [1]; Mickey Mouse and Tinker Bell meet-and-greets (reserved separately); Haunted Mansion; Pirates of the Caribbean; Peter Pan's Flight [2]; Princess Fairytale Hall [8]; The Magic Carpets of Aladdin [7]; Under the Sea–Journey of The Little Mermaid; The Barnstormer [5]; The Many Adventures of Winnie the Pooh [4]; Dumbo the Flying Elephant [6]; Mad Tea Party; Tomorrowland Speedway [3]; Meet Ariel at Her Grotto; "it's a small world" [9]; Monsters, Inc. Laugh Floor; and Mickey's PhilharMagic. Consider the makeup of your group, prioritize your top three attractions, and look for hacks in Chapter 5 and Chapter 6 to make the most of your selections.

129.
Stuffed Animals As Checked Luggage

Someone in your group couldn't resist purchasing a massive Stitch at World of Disney in Disney Springs and now you're lugging around a stuffed toy big enough to take up the seat next to you on the airplane, but fear not: If it fits in the overhead bin, problem solved. If not, ask for a heavy-duty car seat bag when you check in for your flight, label it with your name and address, and send it through as checked luggage. Or, donate it to Toys for Tots or Give Kids The World before you leave.

130.
Newbie Alert: Feet, Boat, or Monorail?

Staying at a Disney resort serviced by the monorail is the ultimate convenience for visiting Magic Kingdom and EPCOT, but sometimes another mode of transportation is the better option. Walking to Magic Kingdom from the Contemporary Resort is faster than making the full Resort monorail circuit, which makes stops at the Transportation and Ticket Center, Polynesian Village Resort, and Grand Floridian Resort before it reaches Magic Kingdom. That also means it's quickest to use the monorail from the Grand Floridian resort to Magic Kingdom. The Polynesian Village Resort is a toss-up; if the monorail is waiting, take it. If the resort's boat hasn't launched, take that instead. Return to these two resorts by resort boat, since the monorail stops at the Contemporary and Transportation and Ticket Center first.

131.
Try the Alternative

The main artery of Interstate 4 links all of Orlando's shopping, dining, and attractions, and while many guests will never venture off Disney property, those who do will benefit from avoiding the interstate's heavy traffic and interminable back-ups. To reach Orlando's other theme parks and attractions, exit Disney property via Buena Vista Drive, which becomes Hotel Plaza Boulevard just beyond Disney Springs. Turn left onto State Road 535, then right onto Palm Parkway. Turn right onto Central Florida Parkway for SeaWorld and Discovery Cove, or keep straight for Universal Orlando. After Palm Parkway becomes Turkey Lake Road, turn right onto Sand Lake Road for the International Drive attractions, or continue to Hollywood Way for Universal Studios, Universal's Islands of Adventure, and Universal's Volcano Bay Water Theme Park.

132.
Keep Your Car Humming

You didn't rent a car at the airport and you've made a last-minute decision to venture beyond Disney. Perhaps you always planned to have a day or two off-site, but don't need a car for your entire vacation. Maybe the car you're using is making strange noises, or the air conditioner stopped working. Don't waste time and money getting to an off-site location. Instead, use Disney's Car Care Center near Magic Kingdom's parking lot, with Alamo and National car rentals and a full-service garage. Need roadside assistance? The Car Care Center can help. It even has a free shuttle for resort pick-up, or for drop-off at Disney's Transportation and Ticket Center, with transportation to Magic Kingdom or EPCOT and bus service to anywhere on Disney property.

133.
Shuttle Your Way to Magic Kingdom

Visitors staying in a Hotel Plaza hotel benefit from a dedicated shuttle that goes directly to each theme park. However, the shuttle only runs every thirty minutes—it stops at each Hotel Plaza resort, and the Magic Kingdom drop-off is at the Transportation and Ticket Center, adding a great deal of time to your journey. If you just missed the shuttle and it's 11:30 a.m. or later, walk to Disney Springs's West Side and catch the Contemporary Resort bus for a twenty-five-minute ride, then walk to Magic Kingdom from there. Prior to 11:30 a.m., the shuttle will take less time. Shopping or dining in Disney Springs after 6 p.m.? A dedicated Hotel Plaza shuttle makes the round-trip until late-night, with departures every thirty minutes.

134.
Use the Resort Monorail

Nothing brings the happy glow of a fabulous day at Magic Kingdom to a grinding halt like the sight of a massive line of people waiting to get on the monorail at the end of the day. The line for the Express monorail, which takes guests directly from Magic Kingdom to the Transportation and Ticket Center, can be absolutely daunting. Instead, take note of the platform signs as you exit the park. There are two monorails from Magic Kingdom: the Resort monorail and the Express monorail. Head straight for the Resort monorail. Although it will make a stop at the Contemporary Resort before it reaches the Transportation and Ticket Center, the line is usually much shorter.

135.
When to Tram and When to Walk

All of the theme parks offer tram service from their massive parking lots (Magic Kingdom trams run from the parking lot to the Transportation and Ticket Center), but sometimes it's quicker to walk than it is to catch a ride. Unless the tram is almost ready to depart from your section, it's quicker to walk from EPCOT's Hei Hei, Moana, and Wall-E lots, and from the front of Crush and Dory. At Hollywood Studios, it's usually quicker to walk from all lots, except for the back half of the farthest lots. Walk from Jafar, Aladdin, Woody, and Zurg, and the front of Hook and Peter Pan for Magic Kingdom. Walk from Unicorn, Peacock, the right-hand side (front) of Butterfly, Dinosaur, and Giraffe at Animal Kingdom.

136.
Nursing Pods

With more than forty million visitors transitioning through each year, Orlando International Airport (MCO) is one of the most family-friendly airports in the country. Not only are there thoughtful touches for children, but it also keeps infants and nursing mothers in mind. Nursing moms who would like a quiet space to feed their babies in comfort and privacy should seek out the Mamava nursing suites, located pre-security on Level 2, post-security in Airsides 1 and 3 near the hub, Airside 2 near gate 111, and near the North Terminal's baggage carousel 24 in Terminal B, Level 2. Each little "room" has a bench seat, outlets for pumping, a small table, and a mirror. The large, white pods aren't immediately obvious as nursing stations, but you can't miss them. There are also private nursing rooms in Airside 4 near gates 20–29 and gate 101.

Thank a Cast Member

Whether you're skipping through the parks on a wave of happiness and sunshine, or you're having one of those days when nothing seems to go right, there is a simple act that will boost your mood: Start thanking the Cast Members. Make a point of thanking ride attendants, bus drivers, boat captains, Mousekeepers, street sweepers, and restroom attendants in particular. Considering what they deal with all day, every day, they don't hear it enough. A genuine "thank you" will make them smile, and in return, it will brighten your day or renew your smile when it's faded. Happiness is contagious.

137.
Save Your Feet with Internal Bus Systems

You forgot to ask for a specific building when making your room requests, and now you're all the way at the back of the resort, seemingly miles from civilization, or at least from the food outlets, bus stops, or pool. If you're staying at one of Disney's largest resorts—Port Orleans, Saratoga Springs, Old Key West, Caribbean Beach, or Coronado Springs—you're in luck. Each of these resorts has its own internal bus system. If you still have time to make non-preferred building requests, ask for:

- Building 3 or 4 at Port Orleans–French Quarter, or Magnolia at Riverside
- Grandstand at Saratoga Springs
- Buildings 11–14 at Old Key West
- Martinique or Trinidad North at Caribbean Beach
- Casitas 1 or Cabanas 9B at Coronado Springs

138.
Reach Animal Kingdom by Bus

Many International Drive hotels have shuttles to Walt Disney World, with relatively easy access to Magic Kingdom, EPCOT, and Hollywood Studios. But what if your hotel doesn't have a shuttle, you're not driving, a taxi or Uber isn't in the budget, and you're trying to get to the hardest-to-reach park of them all, Disney's Animal Kingdom? You're not out of luck. Take the LYNX bus to Disney Springs, catch the bus to Animal Kingdom Lodge, then transfer to the Animal Kingdom bus. It will take time, but it's the most direct route. Don't be tempted to hop on the bus to Coronado Springs. It's "closer" than Animal Kingdom Lodge, but you'll have to make four stops within the resort before moving on to Animal Kingdom.

139.

Morning Express Isn't Always Best

That humongous line waiting to board the monorail at the end of a Magic Kingdom day has a twin, and if you have a dining reservation for a time slot before or just after park opening, you're going to meet that twin. Savvy theme park goers know they need to arrive before park opening, too, and you're going to have plenty of time to get to know them if you line up for the Express monorail. Instead, size up the line for the Resort monorail. If it's much shorter, and it probably will be, chances are you'll arrive at Magic Kingdom sooner by taking that monorail than you would using the Express monorail, even with stops at the Polynesian Village and Grand Floridian resorts.

140.

Split Duties upon Arrival

You've arrived at Orlando International Airport, and all that stands between you and Mickey Mouse is picking up your luggage and your rental car. Rather than hanging around waiting for your bags to arrive, send one adult to baggage claim while the adult who will be driving heads to the car rental counter. All of the major rental companies and their fleets are located on-site. Baggage claim areas for A-Side and B-Side are on Level 2, while ground transportation for each side is on Level 1. There is a good chance your bags will arrive before the car rental agreement is fully filled out, so reunite on Level 1, and you're on your way!

141.
Choose Seats with SeatGuru

Fussy about which seat to choose when booking your flight? Like to know exactly where the restroom is on any given plane, or how close you'll be to the galley or emergency exit? SeatGuru has the answers. Before paying for seats, or while you're comparison-shopping for a flight, visit www.seatguru.com, click on "Seat Maps," enter your chosen airline, date of the flight, and flight number, then click "View Map" when the correct flight shows up. Color-coded seats indicate good, bad, and "be aware" seats, with an explanation of why each received that rating. Amenities and aircraft features are also noted. Additionally, passenger comments let you know exactly what your fellow travelers thought of the legroom, crew, cabin temperature, noise level, and more.

142.
Don't Sweat Parking Lot Closures

You're visiting during one of Walt Disney World's busiest holidays (Fourth of July, Easter, Christmas, or New Year's Eve), and you've been turned away when you reach a theme park parking lot. Don't worry; parking lot closures don't necessarily mean the park is closed to capacity, and chances are you're just being rerouted to an alternate parking location. New Year's Eve crowd levels also necessitate some road closures and detours, so allow up to two hours to navigate Disney property, even if you're not going to a theme park. Planning to watch New Year's Eve fireworks from a Magic Kingdom resort you're not staying in? Grand Floridian, Contemporary, and Polynesian Village's parking lots will be closed to non-resort guests without a dining reservation.

143.
Score One Last Magical Moment

It's been a wonderful vacation. Everything went well, and you wish it never had to end. You've arrived at Orlando International Airport, you've checked your luggage, and it all seems so final. But wait. Before you go through the security checkpoint, indulge in one more Disney moment. Look for the two Magic of Disney stores in the main terminal where you'll be able to pick up last-minute souvenirs and Disney-themed snacks for the flight.

CHAPTER 4

PRACTICAL MATTERS

144.
Newbie Alert: Stop, Look, and Line Up!

You're finally here! Magic Kingdom, EPCOT, Hollywood Studios, or Animal Kingdom looms large, and you cannot wait to charge straight in and get the fun started! But wait. The lines at the entry touch points can be long, even more so between 10 a.m. and noon, so take a moment to scan the length of each line before joining one. People tend to gravitate toward the closest or middle touch point entries first, making lines shorter on both ends. Less savvy guests gravitate toward touch points with people already lined up for them, and you may find an entry with no line. If all entries have lines, quickly scan for lines with few or no children or strollers, two contingencies that tend to slow the process down dramatically.

145.
Use a Backpack

Unless you're a Floridian visiting Disney for the day, you're probably going to bring a bag of stuff into the park. It is much easier to deal with a fanny pack or a backpack than it is to lug around a bag or purse, and your goal is to fit it all into one backpack. Be sure to refill the backpack each night with snacks, admission tickets or MagicBands, and any sundries you need. You don't want to be that person standing at the park entry with a look on her face that says, "I left the tickets back at the hotel." Just add your chilled water bottles in the morning, send one person through bag check while the rest go through the "No Bags" line, and you're on your way! A carabiner or two attached to the outside of your backpack is a great way to carry caps, flip-flops, or nonbreakable purchases to free up space inside the bag. Just make sure they latch securely so nothing slips off.

146.
Photograph Admission Tickets

Every Walt Disney World park admission ticket or MagicBand has a unique twelve-digit identification code located on the back, which Cast Members can use to cancel the ticket or MagicBand if it is lost or stolen. Take a photo of the back of each ticket or write down the code from the back of each MagicBand (it's tiny, and won't show up well in a photo), along with the corresponding user's name. That way, Guest Services can quickly locate the number in their system, cancel the ticket or band, and issue a new one. Disney's system will identify all the stored information, including the number of park admissions remaining, your dining and Genie+ reservations, and any optional information you have linked via My Disney Experience.

147.
Ticket Numbers Are Consecutive— But Still Take That Photo

If you forgot to take a photo of the back of your admission ticket, bring as many other tickets to Guest Services as possible, as long as they were purchased at the same time. It is likely they will be able to figure out the lost ticket number by comparing the numbers on the other tickets you purchased. If they were all purchased at the same time and in the same place, the tickets will have been issued in consecutive order, so it will just be a process of elimination for the Cast Member. That said, take the photo. You can even create a separate album on your cell phone for all of your "useful information" photos.

148.
Newbie Alert: Double-Sided Lines

You're going to stand in a lot of lines over the course of your vacation, so make sure you're not standing in one unnecessarily. It may not be obvious there are two lines at many of the counter-service restaurants. Counter-service locations with cashier stands work on an alternating-sides basis. If everyone ahead of you lined up on one side, get in line on the other side and you'll be served next.

149.
Reunite with Your Lost Camera

There are few things more soul-crushing than discovering you've lost your camera, and along with it all those precious photos you've been taking. Don't be the person calling Disney's Lost and Found every day, or rushing off to the store for an expensive replacement. Before you leave home, write your name and cell phone number on a piece of paper and take a photo of it. If the camera gets lost, the person who finds it (or Guest Services if it's turned in) will know how to contact you to return it. Make sure it's the first picture on your digital card, and remember not to delete it if you download other photos during your stay.

150.
Create a Lost Phone Photo

While you're avoiding a lost camera catastrophe, do your cell phone a favor too. Write your name on a piece of paper, along with the name of your hotel, your email address, and the cell phone number of someone else in your group, if there is one. Take a photo of the paper with your cell phone, then set it as your Lock Screen image so that if your phone is lost the finder will know how to contact you to return it. For added security, do not include information such as your hotel room number or your home address. You will find Lock Screen options under "Settings" on your phone, then follow instructions for choosing an image from your photo gallery.

151.
Give Cast Compliments

You can thank specific Cast Members via the Cast Compliment feature on the My Disney Experience app. Your compliment doesn't have to be anything big or outstanding; if the boat drivers made you laugh with their jokes, Voices of Liberty brought a tear to your eye with their rendition of "America the Beautiful," or the monkey towel animal Mousekeeping left hanging in your room gave you a smile, let them know. Compliments do get passed on, and it will make the Cast Member's day. Remember to include their name and the area where they were working.

152.
Natural Sleep Aids

Having trouble sleeping from all the excitement of being at Walt Disney World? Can't get the kids to calm down for a midday rest after a busy morning in the parks? Eat a banana one hour prior to nap-time or bedtime. Bananas contain potassium and magnesium, which are natural muscle relaxers, but they also contain the amino acid L-tryptophan (the reason you're so sleepy after all that Thanksgiving turkey). Once it hits your brain, science takes over and the L-tryptophan converts to 5-hydroxytryptophan, which then converts to serotonin, and off you go to the Land of Nod, nature's way. Add a glass of warm milk for a double whammy of sleepy goodness!

153.
Stay Hydrated

The two most common reasons for urgent care visits in Orlando are sunburn and heat exhaustion. Florida is subtropical, and it's easy to get sunburned and dehydrated, even in the winter months. It's obvious you'll need a sunscreen of SPF 15 or greater, but by the time you feel thirsty you're already dehydrated. During hotter months, take six big sips of water every fifteen minutes rather than downing a full glass all at once, so that your kidneys can keep up with the added intake. A quick and easy way to tell if you're drinking enough to avoid meeting the doctors at Centra Care Walk-In Urgent Care Center? The "output" from all that water should be clear or very light yellow.

154.
Stay "Regular"

The third most common reason for urgent care visits in Orlando is constipation, especially when it comes to children. They're probably eating more sugar than usual, they're off their regular schedule, and there is so much excitement going on that most kids don't want to take the time for an extended bathroom break—not to mention the shy types who aren't willing to deal with a number two in a public restroom! Pay attention to their "habits" and make sure you provide plenty of time at your accommodation for them to take care of necessities. It's easy to overlook when you're rushing to the parks in the morning, and on the (other) go all day, but it will help you avoid an expensive Centra Care visit for a painful tummy.

155.
Say Goodbye to Foggy Camera Lens

To avoid a foggy camera lens when going between your air-conditioned room and the outdoor heat, put your camera on the balcony or patio for twenty minutes before you leave for the day. That will give it time to defog, but don't forget to take it with you! If you're driving, carry your camera in the trunk of the car so the air conditioning doesn't fog it up again. Take it out of your bag or backpack and remove the lens cap so it defogs faster. In a pinch, carry a microfiber cloth and wipe the lens quickly. You might get a single shot off before it fogs again.

156.
Avoid Inner-Thigh Chafing

Ladies, that cute sundress or flouncy skirt you packed may lead to distress when you're walking around in Florida's heat and humidity all day. Sweat and friction quickly lead to inner-thigh chafing, with a burning rash that can last for days. Take a page out of avid bicyclers' guides and invest a few dollars in an anti-chafing balm such as Body Glide, which rolls on like stick deodorant, is nongreasy, nonstaining, and works like a charm. If restroom stops to reapply don't appeal to you, bring along a pair of lightweight bicycle shorts to wear under your dress and you'll be blissfully chafe-free all day. They wash up easily in your resort sink, and they'll dry overnight.

157.
Be Kind to Your Feet

The average Disney theme park visitor walks approximately ten miles each day, so feet need to be in top condition. Comfortable, broken-in shoes are essential, but even well-loved tootsies will feel the strain after a day or two spent pounding the parks. Bring along an extra pair of socks to change into midday or if your feet get wet, and you'll feel surprisingly rejuvenated. For a serious pick-me-up at the end of the day, treat yourself to a modified foot bath. Sit on the edge of your bathtub and run cold water over your feet for one minute, then hold them under tolerably hot water for one minute, alternating the temperature several times and finishing with one minute of cold. Nearly instant relief!

Get in Shape with Pre-Disney Boot Camp

A Walt Disney World vacation can feel like a military exercise at times, so you're going to want to do some training before heading into "combat." You will lessen the impact of the heat, the walking, and the long days by preparing your body and your mind in advance of your trip. It takes about two weeks to establish a habit, so your goal is to begin your Mickey Training at least that far ahead of your vacation. A month or more is even better.

158. First, start walking. Begin a semi-vigorous walking regimen, aiming to put in an hour or more each day. The further ahead of your trip you can do it, the better. This also gives you the chance to break in new shoes before your feet are really put to the test in the theme parks, and if you can get your family or fellow travelers to join you, everyone will benefit.

159. Increase your water intake. Two weeks before you're due to leave home, start drinking twelve or more twelve-ounce glasses of water, spread out over the course of the day. Preparing your system in advance gives your kidneys time to adjust to a bigger load and become more efficient.

160. Early Theme Park Entry comes early, so if you are staying at a Disney resort and want to take advantage of this perk, get into the habit of waking up early for two weeks before you travel. If you're used to being up by 7 a.m. for work or school, you're all set. If not, remind yourself it will be worth it when you're not waiting for an hour or more in line for Tiana's Bayou Adventure or Expedition Everest–Legend of the Forbidden Mountain because you got to the park during an Early Theme Park Entry morning, or by park opening.

161. Remember, Magic Kingdom can open as early as 8 a.m. (which means 7:30 a.m. for Early Theme Park Entry) during the week between Christmas and New Year's, so plan accordingly if you're visiting during that time frame.

162. While you're preparing yourself for the onslaught, consider the youngest person in the house. Does your baby or toddler only sleep when the house is silent? Start running the vacuum immediately before and during naptime until the drone becomes commonplace and the baby can sleep through it. Then move on to television shows, increasing the volume over the course of a few days. Your little one will be better equipped for a power nap in the parks if everyday sounds are part of their routine.

163. Finally, try to clear your calendar a day or two before your trip so that you can pack your suitcases at a leisurely pace, and get a few early nights. Going into a Disney vacation exhausted because you tried to do too much at the last minute is no way to start a high-energy campaign. Allow time to savor the final stretch, and then let the magic find you!

164.
Activate eTickets at Disney Springs

Unless you arrive in Orlando early enough to get full value from a day's theme park admission, don't wait in the long Guest Services queue at Magic Kingdom, EPCOT, Hollywood Studios, or Animal Kingdom to activate your eTickets or certain Disney Armed Forces Salute tickets. Instead, head directly to Guest Services at Disney Springs and activate them there. The wait will be much shorter, and you'll save a day's admission by exploring the shops and restaurants for the evening. You can also pick up park maps and check for any dining reservations you weren't able to secure before leaving home.

165.
Pro Alert: Share Your Stroller

One of the great joys of the original FastPass system for locals and die-hard Disney fans was the ability to pass on their unused Fast-Passes to guests who would otherwise be waiting in the Standby line. With nontransferable Genie+, that is not possible. However, if you're visiting with young children, you can still create a bit of Disney magic for other guests with kids if you're leaving a park early by passing on your stroller to a family who might need one but hasn't rented one. Watch for families inside the park whose kids look like they're tuckering out. When they go all grateful on you, smile, assure them you're happy to do it, and remind them to "pay it forward."

166.
Avoid Ear Infections

After a full day swimming in the pool or at Blizzard Beach or Typhoon Lagoon, your ears may have that uncomfortable "clogged" feeling, with fuzzy hearing and stuffed-up pressure. Children who spend most of their time underwater are prone to this annoying condition, and the trapped water can lead to a painful bacterial infection if left untreated. If a swimmer can't clear the water by tilting their head to one side and gently tugging on their earlobe, or by opening their mouth as wide as possible, have them try blowing up a balloon. The pressure will help "pop" the ear. If that doesn't work on its own, have them hold their nose while blowing up the balloon.

Extend Your Phone Battery's Charge

Simple setting changes can extend the life of your phone's battery. Disable the flash feature on your camera (Florida is sunny), and use Ringtone instead of Vibrate. Also look for Screen Time-Out, Sleep, Auto-Lock, Low Power Mode, or similar in your settings and select the minimum setting, but be sure you have time to read your Genie+ and dining times if you have them on your Lock Screen or stored as a photo. Reducing the screen's brightness will greatly impact your battery's life. When you're standing outdoors, set it to the lowest possible brightness while still being able to see the screen clearly.

167.
Create Magical Moments for Special Needs

If you are visiting with a guest who has special cognitive needs that may affect their interaction during a character meet-and-greet, inform the character's handler about it before your turn comes, or communicate with the greeter at multi-character locations. They can let the character know and tailor the interaction accordingly. Disney is exceptionally accommodating for guests with special needs, and some of the characters are able to communicate in sign language, as well as tune in to just the right sensitivity so that every guest they meet has an unforgettable experience. Give them a hint and they'll give you their all. Don't forget to have your camera at the ready for some seriously magical moments.

168.
Newbie Alert: Be Flexible

All those plans you made so carefully for months in advance may go straight out the window when you're actually in the theme parks. Plan, plan, plan, and then stop planning. Sometimes over-planning leads to a vacation you (a) hate and (b) don't remember. Even worse, enforcing a rigid schedule upon your loved ones is likely to lead to mutiny. Although much of the true spontaneity of a Disney vacation is a thing of the past, there are really only three things you need to plan for: Genie+ and Individual Lightning Lane times, dining reservations if you choose to make any, and avoiding each park on its busiest day. Then, embrace the freedom that comes from a first visit, when every experience is new and exciting.

169.
Mix and Match MagicBands

Each MagicBand is linked to the individual who will use it, but only the center "icon" (disc) contains their information. The standard MagicBands come in eight solid colors, so if you have nine or more in your group and same-color bands will cause confusion, you can mix and match colors. The center icon can be removed using an eyeglass repair–sized screwdriver and placed inside a band of another color. Swap colors to stand out from the average Disney goer, let your artistic side shine through, or, if you're visiting over Christmas, request half of your MagicBands in green and half in red, then swap out the icons and go full-on festive.

170.
Upgrade to MagicBand+

MagicBand+ is MagicBand's tech-savvy younger sibling. The updated wearables do everything MagicBands can do (open on-property resort hotel room doors, charge purchases, and scan into park entrances and Lightning Lanes), but also have interactive features within the parks, and they light up during nighttime spectaculars. They also require charging and, of course, cost more.

171.
Make My Disney Experience Your Lock Screen

As a Disney vacationer, you'll use your phone's camera a lot. To help conserve battery power, open up the My Disney Experience app on your cell phone and take a screenshot of your daily schedule. To take a screenshot on an Android phone, hold down the Power and Volume Down buttons simultaneously, watch for the screen to "shrink" momentarily, and the screenshot will show up in your notifications tray or the Screenshots folder. On an iPhone, hold the Right Side and Volume Up buttons. Models with TouchID vary, but you'll find instructions in your manual or online. Locate the photo, make it your Lock Screen picture for the day, and you'll have your Genie+ times and dining reservation information available without logging on and burning through your battery.

172.
Avoid Sadness with Refunds and Replacements

Disasters happen, even at Walt Disney World. Entire ice creams plop onto the pavement, brand-new souvenirs break, and that Goofy hat you were so excited about ten minutes ago looks like a goofy hat when you catch sight of your reflection in a window. Instead of wallowing in sadness or buyer's remorse, bring your receipt to the shop or kiosk from which you purchased the item and it will be cheerfully refunded or replaced. If your child's balloon pops—even if it was the consequence of her experimenting with something sharp coming in contact with Mickey's helium-filled head—bring the flat, tattered remains to any Cast Member selling balloons and they will save the day by sending your youngster off with a new one.

173.
Use Thunderstorms to Your Advantage

To your horror, the weather forecast is "50 percent chance of rain" every single day of your vacation. If that's the case, you're probably traveling during the summer months, when afternoon thunderstorms are common. First, don't fret; Florida storms are so quirky that it can rain at Magic Kingdom and be perfectly dry at EPCOT. Prime thunderstorm territory is 3 p.m. to 6 p.m., so save long indoor attractions, such as Enchanted Tales with Belle, Spaceship Earth, For the First Time in Forever: A Frozen Sing-Along, or Festival of the Lion King, until you know when the rain will arrive.

174.
Capture the Moment Your Beloved Says "Yes!"

You've been planning a surprise Disney engagement for months. The ring has been purchased, the words have been rehearsed, and you're in the theme park that means so much to both of you. Before you get down on one knee, and without your "intended" hearing, quickly whisper, "I'm proposing," to the PhotoPass photographer when your turn arrives. If you inform Guest Services ahead of time regarding where you'll propose and what time you plan to be there, they can make sure a photographer is on hand to capture the special moment. When the joyful "Yes" has been said and happy bystanders have wished you well, take a final photo that includes your PhotoPass photographer, and post it on Facebook using #CastCompliments. If you want to include characters in your magical proposal, keep in mind they can't be "actively" involved, which means as much as he probably wants to, Mickey can't hold the ring.

175.
Download the Shop Disney App

Forgot to purchase a special souvenir before your vacation ended? Want to send Disney merchandise home? Download the free Shop Disney app from the App Store or Google Play, and select the items you would like to purchase. If you're still in a theme park, you can check the app for a nearby shop that carries the item. Standing in a shop but don't want to lug merchandise around with you all day? Scan the item's barcode and put it in your online basket. When you're ready to purchase, you can choose to have your selections sent to your Disney resort, or have them sent home (United States addresses only). Even better? Annual Passholder, Disney Vacation Club, and Disney Visa cardholder discounts all apply.

Ask about Disability Access Service

Guests with visible and nonvisible disabilities that prevent them from queuing can request Disability Access Service (DAS), which allows them to schedule return times for the attractions. Use your first return time, then visit a second attraction to schedule a return time, and so on. DAS can be used along with Genie+, and only one DAS registration is needed for all four theme parks. Wheelchair and scooter users don't need to register for DAS because queues are wide enough to accommodate them, but all guests with accessibility concerns can visit Guest Services and ask about available options for their specific needs.

176.
Hack a Selfie Stick Replacement

Selfie sticks are banned from all Walt Disney World parks, but that doesn't mean you can't get those long-distance photos everyone loves so much. Clip-on, wide-angle lenses are inexpensive, small, and practically weightless. They fit most cell phones, and they're easy to use (simply clip the lens over your phone's lens). Although long-reaching sticks are not allowed, their shorter brethren, "tabletop" or mini tripods, are still acceptable. Find a wall, trash bin, railing, or other structure on which to stabilize your mini tripod, set the photo timer, jump into the shot, and snap away. The ultimate "selfie stick"? You'll never be short of other Disney guests who are willing to take your photo. Just ask, and be sure you offer to take theirs too!

177.
Fend Off the Adult Meltdown Hour

If you're traveling with children you probably jumped straight to Chapter 9, and now you know all about the four o'clock meltdown hour. Don't get all smug if you're not visiting with human sirens, though. Five o'clock is "adult meltdown hour," and if you've been park-pounding for three or more days, you're going to participate. Pop into a tucked-away lounge, such as Tutto Gusto Wine Cellar or the outdoor patio at Tiffins Restaurant, or seek out a quiet spot along the short, "hidden" walkway between Storybook Circus and TRON Lightcycle/Run in Magic Kingdom; United Kingdom's back garden in EPCOT (if the band isn't playing); the walkway immediately outside Star Wars: Galaxy's Edge that leads to Toy Story Land at Hollywood Studios; or the area behind Flame Tree Barbecue in Animal Kingdom. Best remedy? Ditch the regimented schedule. It works wonders.

Use Ziploc Bags

The best thing you can pack for your Orlando vacation, after your credit card and toothbrush, is a stash of Big Bag, gallon, storage, sandwich, and snack-sized Ziploc bags. They add next to no weight, they take up very little space in your suitcase, and you can store the smaller bags in the larger bags while you're in transit. They are likely to get tattered with use, so bring along a few of each size.

178. Long road trips to reach Orlando can bring on a wicked case of back-seat sibling rivalry. Pack a gallon-sized Ziploc bag with nonperishable snacks, write each child's name on their bag, and enjoy no more fighting over who ate whose brownie, or who hogged the last baggie of Cheetos.

179. Use a sandwich-sized bag to store items such as miniature bubbles (find them in the wedding section of your local craft store), a loop of string to play Cat's Cradle, or cards from games such as Taboo, Taboo Junior, or Trivial Pursuit in one place to entertain children while waiting in noninteractive queues. Add a handful of rubber bands to keep items such as game cards tidy.

180. Reasonably priced dry bags made specifically for cell phones are readily available, but Ziploc bags will keep your phone dry at a fraction of the cost. Slip it into a sandwich-sized bag to keep it dry on water rides, in the rain, or when tending to children playing in the pop-jet splash pads in EPCOT and Disney Springs. If you hold the bag tight against the phone you will still be able to use its camera feature.

181. If the day isn't warm enough to dry children's wet clothing after playing in a splash area (or damp socks, if you're changing them at midday to help avoid blisters), bring along dry clothes in a large Ziploc bag. When it's time to change, put the wet items into the bag and carry them in your backpack without getting everything else damp.

182. Assemble a full outfit of children's clothes for each day of your vacation, and put them in individual gallon-sized Ziploc bags before packing them in your suitcase. You'll have a ready-made outfit each morning so that preschoolers can dress themselves. Pack one extra bag with a change of clothing and add it to your backpack for use during your days in the parks, in case of spills or impromptu play in a splash area.

183. In the event you have forgotten to bring a bottle of sanitizing spray with you to clean germy areas of your resort room, you can still avoid touching the grimiest thing in the room, the television remote control. Turn a storage-sized bag inside out, pick the remote up using the inside of the bag, then fold the bag right-side out again. No cross-contamination, no germy hands when you use it, and you can toss the bag into the trash at the end of your vacation.

184.
Take Advantage of Same-Day Deliveries

No need to visit the grocery store for nonperishable food or bottled water. Amazon Prime members enjoy free same-day deliveries to their home address, but that convenient service also applies to their accommodation in Orlando. Visit https://primenow.amazon.com, log in to your account, and confirm delivery is available to your accommodation by entering its zip code into the "Shopping In" drop-down box. Select your items (must total $20 or more); enter your address (include your name and the word "guest" after your resort name and before the street address); choose your delivery time; add your mobile number, any special instructions, payment method, and billing address; then place your order. Packages, with the exception of alcohol, will be left at the front desk until you return.

185.
Use Flat Rate Shipping

In the excitement of your Disney vacation, you've done the unthinkable. You've purchased more souvenirs than you have room for in your suitcase, and now you're facing the hard realities of airline luggage allowances. You could spring for a new case and bite the bullet on airline fees, or you could drop by the Sand Lake Post Office, four miles from Walt Disney World, and pick up a free Flat Rate box. Items that fit into Flat Rate boxes can be shipped to US destinations for under $20, depending on box size. If the items don't fit, your clothes certainly will. Roll up enough clothes to make room, stuff them into the smallest Flat Rate box possible, and let the postal service do the rest.

186.
Make a Q-tip Quick Fix

Photographs make treasured mementos from any Disney vacation, and you're going to take a lot of them. If you need a new memory card, batteries, or a disposable camera, the Camera Center in EPCOT has you covered. But what if something goes wrong? While major repairs require a professional, there are quick fixes for two of the most common problems. Auto-focus getting sluggish or not working? Clean the contacts on your lens and camera body with a Q-tip and isopropyl alcohol, both of which can be purchased at any drugstore or supermarket for just a few dollars. Grungy camera lens? Clean the front and back of the lens with a Q-tip and isopropyl alcohol, then wipe them vigorously with your microfiber cloth. Problem solved!

187.
Bring a Reusable Bag

Disney has long been a leader in responsible recycling programs. While the removal of single-use plastics is great news for the environment, there is one pesky plastic whose elimination may catch visitors by surprise. Plastic merchandise bags are a thing of the past in the Disney parks, and that means planning ahead if your visit will include shopping. Reusable bags can be purchased for a reasonable price in Walt Disney World, but you probably have a lightweight, reusable bag in a closet at home. Bring one along for purchases that are too large to fit in your backpack.

188.
Talk to a Manager

Something has gone wrong, and now a guest is upset, unhappy, and yelling at a Cast Member in an attempt to get justice. Berating the frontline workers rarely ends well, so don't be that person. Instead, make certain the problem you're dealing with is truly a problem (being asked to remove a child from your shoulders during a parade isn't a problem; it's a safety issue), ask to speak with a manager, explain your issue, and wait for a solution. Don't fume about it and send an angry email when you return home. Instead, give the Cast Member or manager the chance to make it right as soon as the problem arises. They might even throw in a little something to make you smile again.

189.
Find Relief at the First Aid Centers

Bumps, cuts, and headaches are standard fare at First Aid, but a visit to a licensed nurse isn't the only service available. Along with sample sizes of over-the-counter medications and basic medical care, guests will find less obvious items, including foot-care necessities and blister relief; mini tools for fixing glasses or sunglasses; cleansing solution for contact lenses; thermometer strips for taking temperatures; sewing kits for minor clothing repairs; and in an emergency, EpiPens. Guests who need to keep their insulin or other medications refrigerated are welcome to use First Aid's coolers, and there are safety boxes for disposing of hypodermic needles. Forgot the wax for your dental braces? You'll find some at First Aid too. Best of all? It's free.

190.
Avoid the Disney Rash

After walking miles in the Florida heat and humidity, park-goers may experience a red, itchy rash, and swelling around their ankles. This is the dreaded "Disney Rash" (yes, it's actually called that, but the medical term is exercise-induced vasculitis, and don't worry, it's harmless, if annoying). Cold compresses and elevating your feet at the end of each day can alleviate the symptoms, but over-the-counter topical medications can also help curb the itch.

191.
Plan the Ultimate Photo Session for Your Big Event

Planning to propose and want to capture every blissful second? Finally getting the whole family together for a magical vacation? Whatever your special event, Disney's added-fee Capture Your Moment private photo sessions provide memories that will last forever. Purchase Memory Maker or an Annual Pass with Memory Maker add-on and your photos will be free!

192.
Soothe Sunburns

You may not be afflicted with the condition hemorrhoid cream was created for, but if you've been careless with your sun protection, nearby drugstores and grocery stores have just what you need. Pick up a couple of tubes of Preparation H and slather it over your sunburn. It contains an anesthetic to lessen the pain and ingredients that help shrink your poor, swollen tissues. Grab a bottle of alcohol-free aloe vera gel while you're in the store, and chill it in your mini fridge for added cooling relief. If you overindulge in the Fiesta Margaritas while you're on vacation, Preparation H won't cure your hangover, but a tiny dab will lessen the bags under your eyes.

193.
Never Lose a Pin

Pin trading at Walt Disney World began in 1999 during the Millennium Celebration as a means of bringing guests together and has been going strong ever since, although most trading now happens between guests and Cast Members. However, the rubber Mickey-head backings aren't the most reliable, and it's easy to lose a favorite pin during the course of your day. In an emergency, barrel-shaped earring backs fit some pins. When you return home, purchase bulk bullet clutch earring backs from Michaels or Amazon. Specialized locking backs available at Michaels or on Amazon are best, but they require a tool and a lot of fiddling; not ideal when making a trade. Worst case? Pop the eraser off a pencil and use that as a temporary backing (this also works for lost earring backs).

194.

Rescue Your Specs with Sunglass Saver

Want to wear your sunnies on a roller coaster, but you're afraid they'll fly away? Fear no more. Inexpensive adjustable glasses straps available on Amazon will ensure your eyewear's safety. And since they come in multipacks, you'll have extras to hold prescription glasses in place on indoor wild rides.

195.

Chew Ginger Candy for an Upset Stomach

That roller coaster or motion simulator you just rode didn't agree with your tummy. All that sugary and fatty food you've been eating is causing an uproar. Maybe the day is extra hot and you just downed a big cup of ice water, which isn't the best idea when your body temperature is up. Or, you're having so much fun you didn't stop for nourishment, and now you're having massive hunger pangs halfway through the Avatar Flight of Passage queue. Add a package of chewy ginger candies to your backpack for quick upset stomach relief. Suck on a candy for motion sickness, eat one before drinking ice water on a hot day, or use the candy to get you to your next meal without a gurgling belly.

196.
Locate Companion Restrooms

Guests who require extra personal assistance will find Companion Restrooms (sometimes called Family Restrooms) clearly marked on each theme park map, with a symbol featuring a wheelchair along with the standard man and woman figures that denote restrooms. They are larger than disability-friendly stalls, which are not ideal if your wheelchair includes a tray. Although these specialized restrooms do provide changing tables for children, there are no changing tables suitable for adults in any Walt Disney World restroom. When the situation requires additional accommodation for adult care, drop in at any of the First Aid centers and request the use of a private room. Large, comfortable rooms are available without charge, and they are purpose-designed to offer an added level of privacy, convenience, and accessibility for guests and caregivers.

Know the Lingo

Some of the terms you'll hear at Walt Disney World are fairly obvious, such as Cast Member (employee), costume (uniform), and backstage (the part of the parks guests can't see). Less obvious terms include Code 101 (ride breakdown), Code 102 (ride restarting), "friend of" (performer who "plays" a character, as in, "I'm a friend of Cinderella"), and the creepiest one of all, "White Powder Alert" (a guest, usually riding Haunted Mansion, has just sprinkled their dearly departed's ashes inside the attraction, meaning they committed a crime), which leads to "E-Stop" (emergency stop and possible evacuation of the ride). Fun, hey?

197.
Give Kids the World

If your vacation was so fantastic you wish everybody could experience the Disney magic, this one is for you. Give Kids The World is Orlando's most beloved organization, providing children with life-threatening illnesses (and their families) the chance to make their wish for a Disney trip come true. While direct donations help make that possible, donating lightly used items, such as that stroller you purchased or the gigantic stuffed animal you won, helps too. Profits from the sale of those items go directly to Give Kids The World. You can even create a Disney challenge and raise sponsorship money while you play in the parks, or "donate your birthday" and request contributions in lieu of gifts. Set up a page at www.gktw.org, let your friends know about it, and the organization will do the rest!

CHAPTER 5

THEME PARKS
LIKE
A PRO

198.
Make the Most of Park Hopping

If your theme park ticket includes park hopping, choose your morning park wisely to maximize your time. Start at Magic Kingdom, which has the most attractions, then hop to another park in the afternoon. Or, start at Hollywood Studios if Magic Kingdom isn't a priority. There is an exception, though: If you're trying for an Individual Lightning Lane attraction at one of the parks, prioritize that park.

199.
Become a Galactic Hero

Those thousands of hours you or your kids spend playing *Kingdom Hearts* or *World of Warcraft* ought to pay off somehow, and Buzz Lightyear's Space Ranger Spin is the place to put your skills to the test. If you prove to be a true galactic hero (meaning, you scored 999,999 points and the level you're awarded at the end of your ride is, in fact, "Galactic Hero"), take a quick photo of your score as you pass by the scoreboard near the end of the ride and present it at the photo desk. You'll be rewarded with a special sticker announcing your awesome new status within the universe, which gives you bragging rights literally forever.

200.
Cancel Unnecessary Genie+

You made the ultimate rookie mistake and booked a Genie+ selection for an attraction that rarely has a long queue, such as Finding Nemo: The Big Blue... and Beyond!; Monsters, Inc. Laugh Floor; Muppet*Vision 3D; or Mickey's PhilharMagic. Or, maybe you arrived at your Genie+ attraction only to find there was no queue. Stop a moment before you enter the attraction and take a look at the current Genie+ options on your My Disney Experience app. If something you like has opened up, and you're certain you don't want a second visit to experience the attraction you're ditching, cancel or modify your existing Genie+ time and select the new one. Remember, if you've purchased an Individual Lightning Lane, that return time cannot be canceled or modified.

201.
Take a Free Drawing Class

Scoring a job as a Disney artist might be beyond most guests' skill level, but learning to draw the characters with surprising accuracy is well within reach. Guests visiting Disney's Animal Kingdom park can take part in one of The Animation Experience at Conservation Station's free drawing classes, and channel their inner Imagineer. Twenty-five-minute classes with step-by-step instructions on how to draw a Disney character are offered daily, with the first class starting at 10 a.m. and the last class starting at 4:45 p.m., with times subject to change. Classes are kid-friendly, and you get to keep your drawing.

202.
Pro Alert: Children's Finger Scans

All guests over the age of three are required to provide a fingerprint scan and tap their park pass or MagicBand at the front gate of each theme park or water park. Scanners can be quirky, making wiggly fingers difficult to scan, and some youngsters are not exactly cooperative with the procedure. In addition, some parents prefer not to have their child's details placed in Disney's database. Happily, you have a choice. Adults who have concerns about little fingers using the scanners can use their own fingerprints. Choose one adult in your group to be the official "fingerprint" when activating a child's ticket. Be aware, the fingerprint associated with the child's ticket must be used each time the child enters a park.

203.
Seek Out Overlapping Genie+ Times

Often, the most popular attractions won't have Genie+ availability for a group of three or more, but at times may be available if you search for them individually. Try selecting one guest at a time and search for overlapping return windows within the same hour. If you are able to find enough to cover your entire group, you will be able to ride together during the time frame that overlaps. If you still can't work out a schedule that includes everyone, consider booking for as many in your party as you can, and try for the next-closest time slot for the rest of the group.

204.
Take a Shortcut

When navigating crowded parks, sometimes a shortcut will get you from point A to point B quicker than the most obvious and direct route. Try using Magic Kingdom's path between Storybook Circus and Tomorrowland, and the boardwalk running along Rivers of America between Haunted Mansion and Tiana's Bayou Adventure; the walkway between Test Track and Mexico, and the rose garden path between World Celebration and World Showcase in EPCOT; and Animal Kingdom's paths between Africa and Pandora–The World of Avatar, the pathways circling around the Tree of Life, or cut through the shops in Discovery Island when heading into Pandora. Hollywood Studios' convoluted walkways have no shortcuts, but you can cut the corner off by walking through The Trolley Car Café to get to Sunset Boulevard.

205.
Navigate in Single File

Sometimes the simplest ideas have the biggest impact, and that is certainly the case when it comes to getting through theme park crowds quickly. While longtime visitors develop a sixth sense when they are navigating the parks and are mentally geared up to veer around guests who stop without warning, or scoot past groups who walk at a snail's pace and appear oblivious to their surroundings, one easy trick will help even novice visitors get from point A to point B like pros. Ignore your natural inclination to walk side by side, and walk single file instead. You'll be amazed at how much faster your group will move through the crowds. Make sure children walk in the middle of the row so no one is left behind.

206.
Score the Perfect Signature

There are two types of Disney characters in the parks: face characters and head characters. Anna and Elsa, Cinderella, Peter Pan, and Tinker Bell are characters with human faces, with complete range of movement and the ability to carry on a conversation. Chip and Dale, the Beast, and Tigger are fully costumed head characters (also known as "furries") who communicate only with their hands and their body movements. Head characters' vision is limited, and their hands tend to be gloved or oversized, making it difficult (in some cases, impossible) to hold a pen or thin marker when signing autograph books. Bring along a Sharpie or a thick pen for them to use and you'll be rewarded with an easy-to-read signature.

207.
Newbie Alert: Use Left-Hand Queues

Many attractions have a right-hand queue and a left-hand queue, separated by a barrier. As you enter the attraction, take a quick look at which queue appears to be longer. It's a time-tested strategy to use the left-hand queue, as most guests gravitate naturally to the right, and the left-hand queue is often shorter, sometimes considerably so. If one of the two queues is not in use, it will be roped off or a Cast Member will be in place to direct you to the open queue. But if it's open, get in it! Be sure you don't mistake the Genie+/Lightning Lane queue for the Standby queue. Each will be clearly marked at the entry to the attraction.

208.
Bring Treats for Cast Members

Bring wrapped mini candy canes or other seasonal, wrapped treats to give to Cast Members who are working over a major holiday such as Independence Day, Halloween, Thanksgiving, Christmas, or New Year's Eve. Unlike Mousekeeping or restaurant servers and bartenders, Cast Members can't accept tips or "big" gifts, so small, inexpensive treats show them you appreciate the time they're spending away from family celebrations to ensure guests have a magical vacation, and doing it with a smile and a great attitude. Thank them with a kind word and a sweet treat, and remember, street sweepers and restroom attendants are often forgotten in favor of more prominent frontline workers, even though their efforts keep the parks so visually appealing.

209.
Hack a Coin Holder

In most places, coins thrown into a fountain are a nuisance. At Walt Disney World, they're a gift. Treat the kids (or yourself) to M&M's Minis that come in a plastic tube and you'll have a ready-made container for carrying around loose change you can toss into fountains, themed wells, and in-park water features, especially the water around the queue at the "it's a small world" attraction and the wishing well along the pathway between Cinderella Castle and Fairytale Garden in Magic Kingdom's Fantasyland. Disney collects the coins and uses them toward an annual donation that aids needy children throughout central Florida. Those nickels and dimes really add up, so toss away—and don't forget to make a wish!

210.
Fill In Some Great Service Fanatic Cards

Experience a magical moment with a Cast Member? Drop in at any Guest Services and fill in a Great Service Fanatic Card. Disney is terrific about recognizing Cast Members who go that extra mile, and it's a serious mood booster when a manager shows up with praise for a job well done. While these recognitions are coveted by all Cast Members, it is especially true for ride attendants and other "routine" positions that often go unnoticed. The cards become part of the Cast Member's personal file, and they can go a long way for those trying to advance their career with the Mouse. You're not only doing something nice for them in the short term; your comments may have a long-term positive influence.

211.
Draw Pictures for Favorite Characters

One of the most touching gifts a character can receive is a hand-made note or picture from a guest. Have kids (or kids at heart) draw a picture of their favorite character, park, or attraction—or color in a page from a coloring book if the child is very young—and present it to the character during your meet-and-greet. Personalized, handcrafted works of art, specific to the character, are the kind of treasured mementos that show you're thinking of them even before you arrive, and they are kept as treasured remembrances when Mickey's friends move on to adventures beyond their time at Walt Disney World.

Get Creative with Character Autographs

Collecting autographs is one of the high points of a Disney vacation for many guests, and there are creative ways to collect and display your favorite characters' signatures.

212. **Create a unique gift for the youngsters in your life by purchasing a selection of Little Golden Books featuring classic Disney stories,** and have the relevant character sign the title page in each one. Be sure to have the book open to the page you want signed when your turn comes, especially with head characters who may not be able to turn the pages.

213. **Purchase a sturdy, white photo mat with a wide border and have each character you meet sign it with a colorful marker,** then insert a special family photo from your vacation when you return home. If you don't mind the extra weight in your backpack, bring along a selection of colored markers for the most festive-looking end product, and be sure to store the mat in a large, sealable bag to keep it clean and dry while you tour.

214. **Pick up a 4 × 6 photo album with double-sided sleeves, and a pack of 4 × 6 index cards.** Have each character you meet sign one card, and display it in the album opposite a photo of you with the character. Remember to take along something solid, such as a lightweight book or small clipboard, so the character has a firm base on which to sign the card.

215. **Characters are allowed to sign clothing, but only if you're not wearing it at the time.** T-shirts make good signature canvases, as do baseball hats. Disney-themed pillowcases are another fun option. Be sure to use a permanent fabric pen so you don't lose the autograph the first time it goes through the wash.

216.
Estimate Meet-and-Greet Times

Characters generally interact with guests for about twenty to thirty minutes per "set" if they're outdoors, or thirty to forty-five minutes if their meet-and-greet is indoors. Every character has a handler, so if the line to meet them is formidable, ask the handler how much longer the character will be out. Characters typically spend between two and three minutes with each group, so count the number of groups in front of you before entering the queue, and tally up an approximate wait time, including an additional minute to account for any unexpected love-fest compliments of that overexcited four-year-old ahead of you. If it appears the character will take a break before you meet her or him, return in early evening when lines are shorter.

Pop-Up Characters

Like all Disney performers, even the characters have to undergo training, and EPCOT is the place to be for their pop-up meet-and-greets. You won't find them in your My Disney Experience app; they'll just show up unexpectedly and it's your chance to meet some of the rarer characters, often with little or no wait. Watch for them along the short street to the left of The American Adventure, and between the Canada and United Kingdom pavilions. Some of the characters include Tarzan and Jane, Pinocchio, Geppetto, Jiminy Cricket, Robin Hood, Evil Queen, and Mushu.

217.
No Plastic Lids or Straws

Walt Disney World has phased out plastic cup lids and straws, in an effort to reduce landfill waste. You can request a paper straw at the parks, but they tend to get mushy quickly and are difficult for toddlers to use. If you have a youngster who isn't proficient with a large, open cup filled with liquid, bring along a sippy cup or reusable mug with a lid so that they don't end up with soaking-wet clothes and a wasted drink. Do not save a plastic straw from a previous drink purchase and bring it into Animal Kingdom. They pose a serious health risk to the animals when they (invariably) find their way into an enclosure. Reusable metal or bamboo straws are also great eco-friendly options and can be washed between uses.

218.
Enjoy a Dripless Mickey

One of the most iconic treats at Walt Disney World is Mickey's Premium Ice Cream Bar on a stick. One of the least pleasant experiences is having it drip down your arm while you're eating it. Disney no longer has plastic cup lids, so how do you stop the drips from melting treats? Pop into a counter-service restaurant and ask for a small paper plate. Then, punch a slit in the middle of the plate with your car key or other semi-sharp implement, stick the ice cream's handle into the slot with the plate's rim pointing upward, and enjoy a cooling snack, drip-free.

219.
Newbie Alert: Save Time with Single Rider Lines

If only one person in your group wants to ride an attraction, or group members don't mind splitting up, use the Single Rider queue to reduce wait times. While there is a small possibility two in your group will be seated in the same ride vehicle, it is far more likely they won't, so be certain children are okay with the idea of riding with strangers. Requests to ride together once you reach the boarding area will be met with a polite but firm refusal. Attractions that offer the Single Rider option are Test Track at EPCOT, Expedition Everest–Legend of the Forbidden Mountain at Animal Kingdom, and Rock 'n' Roller Coaster Starring Aerosmith and Millennium Falcon: Smuggler's Run at Hollywood Studios.

220.
Find a Quiet Retreat

First Aid centers aren't just for health- or injury-related matters. They also provide a low-stimulation environment in which to de-stress for guests with cognitive disabilities. If a quiet courtyard or seldom-used pathway in each park isn't enough, drop in at First Aid and request a quiet room. You'll find First Aid tucked away on the side street between Casey's Corner and The Crystal Palace in Magic Kingdom; in the Odyssey Events Pavilion in World Showcase at EPCOT; in the Guest Relations courtyard near the information kiosk closest to Sid Cahuenga's One-of-a-Kind shop at Hollywood Studios; and next to Creature Comforts in Discovery Island at Disney's Animal Kingdom. Blizzard Beach and Typhoon Lagoon have First Aid centers too.

221.
Keep Your Feet Dry

If you get caught in an unexpected downpour and end up with soaking-wet shoes, two large Ziploc bags can save your feet if your shoes are still wet the next morning. Stuff one bag into each shoe so that the bag is open at the top and you can slip your foot into it. That will keep your socks dry until the day's heat dries out your shoes.

What Is "DisneyBound"?

Guests over the age of thirteen are not allowed into the parks dressed as Disney characters. Instead, fans participate in DisneyBound by dressing in a way that "suggests" the character without "replicating" the character. To join in, think about the colors the character you'd like to represent wears, and what their "vibe" is (hip, dorky, retro), and use those as your inspiration. Don't take their costume literally; boots can be tennis shoes, a princess ball gown can be a skirt and top. DisneyBounding isn't limited to walk-around characters, either; the iconic elements of the attractions are fun to honor too!

222.
Do Mickey's Halloween Party for "Free"

If you want to experience the atmosphere of Mickey's Not-So-Scary Halloween Party without purchasing a ticket, position yourself at the back of Magic Kingdom before closing time and dawdle in each land before you're required to move on. You will be asked to proceed through each land between you and the Hub until you're filtered directly down Main Street, U.S.A. and out of the park, but you'll get to see guests in their Halloween costumes, which is pretty magical. Just remember: Don't argue with Cast Members as they urge you along, and don't try to access an attraction. You're on borrowed theme park time and they're only doing their job, so be grateful and pleasant as you make your way out.

223.
Get an Overlooked World Showcase Souvenir

World Showcase at EPCOT has a wealth of unique shops to browse, with gifts and merchandise you won't find anywhere else at Walt Disney World. One of the best souvenirs, though, is also one of the most overlooked. Along with collecting character signatures in your autograph book, stop at the Morocco, China, and Japan pavilions and ask a Cast Member to sign your book. It's a fun diversion if they're not busy, and they'll add your name (or your child's name) as it would be written in their country's language and alphabet. Many World Showcase Cast Members are on an international exchange program for up to a year, and a few minutes' conversation about their culture makes a nice reminder of home.

224.
Don't Lose Your MagicBand

Bitbelt watchband loops were originally created to keep Fitbit activity trackers in place, but they work equally well to keep your MagicBand or MagicBand+ from snapping open and falling off your wrist. Simply slide the silicone band over the receiver end of the strap (the one with holes in it), snap the connecter end of the strap into the holes, then slide the Bitbelt over the connector end for a safer fit.

225.
Maintain Modesty on Summit Plummet

For convenience and modesty, it's best to wear a one-piece bathing suit when riding Summit Plummet at Blizzard Beach Water Park. The force of the water on this powerful slide is known for removing the top portion of a bikini on the way down, and it may arrive at the bottom of the slide at a time that does not coincide with the time the wearer (more accurately, former wearer) arrives. Ladies, plan your swimwear accordingly and avoid unhappiness and embarrassment once you reach the bottom.

226.
Hydrate at the Water Parks

Dehydration can quickly become a big problem during a water-park day, so be sure to stay hydrated at Blizzard Beach and Typhoon Lagoon. It's easy to fool yourself into thinking you're not thirsty with all that water around you, and the fact you're cooler than you would be in a theme park, but it's even easier to get dehydrated there, considering all the stairs you'll be climbing to get to the tops of the slides. Take time after each slide to slurp down a few big gulps of water, and if you have children with you, keep track of their intake too. Don't worry about needing the restroom too often. You'll be sweating out nearly as much liquid as you take in.

227.
Newbie Alert: When in Doubt, Get in Line!

Maybe you didn't spend months planning your Walt Disney World vacation. Maybe you figured you could just "wing it" once you got there. Or maybe your plans got blown out of the water by rain, a cranky kid, a ride shutting down, too many Shrunken Zombie Head cocktails at Trader Sam's last night, or maybe you just needed to sleep in for a change. Whatever the reason, you're now wandering around the park in a daze, overwhelmed and unsure what to do next. Instead of standing in the middle of the walkway looking at your park map and deciding what to do, get in line at a nearby attraction. By the time you've mapped out a new plan, you could be at the front of the queue.

Strategize Genie+

The makeup of your group and the way you most enjoy touring the parks will have a big impact on how you use Genie+. There is no "right" way to use it, but there are strategies that will help make the most of the system and make your time in the parks more enjoyable.

228. **The first two hours of the day are the slowest, and most attractions will not have long wait times.** The exceptions are Avatar Flight of Passage, Seven Dwarfs Mine Train, Frozen Ever After, Toy Story Mania!, Slinky Dog Dash, Remy's Ratatouille Adventure, the attractions in Star Wars: Galaxy's Edge, plus Guardians of the Galaxy: Cosmic Rewind and TRON Lightcycle/Run (once Standby is available).

229. **If you start your park day early (and the parks aren't excessively busy),** you should be able to "stack" Genie+ attractions one right after the other with no large time gaps in-between.

230. **If your Genie+ return time is more than two hours away,** you can make a second reservation two hours after making the first (Genie will let you know when you can book).

231. **If you head straight to the back of the park upon arrival,** you can get ahead of parkgoers who stop closer to the entrance. Then you can work your way back once crowds disperse.

232. **Your group *can* select different Genie+ attractions,** which is a big bonus if you're visiting with children of varying ages or interests. Have one adult schedule a Genie+ time for a tamer, preschooler-friendly attraction that doesn't interest the older child, while another adult schedules a thrill ride with an older child during the same time slot. Mix and match who goes with whom so everyone gets a fair shake at the rides they'll most enjoy.

233.
Be the Last to Leave

If you think you've seen heavy crowds during the day, you're in for a real surprise when it's time to leave the parks and board a bus or take to the roadways at the end of the day. Instead of rushing out with the masses, let the majority fight to get out while you linger for thirty minutes enjoying some of the lesser-known "extras" most guests will never see. At Magic Kingdom, don't miss the Kiss Goodnight. Along with the music to "When You Wish Upon a Star," it includes a lovely "Thank you for visiting" voice-over as Cinderella Castle twinkles with fairy lights.

234.
Don Ponchos on Water Rides

There is nearly always one person in the group who refuses to get wet on Tiana's Bayou Adventure in Magic Kingdom or Kali River Rapids in Animal Kingdom. Keep him or her happy (and relatively dry) by tucking a lightweight Walmart or dollar store rain poncho into your backpack, so she or he can cover up after boarding the log or raft. Although cheap ponchos are extremely thin, they'll survive a few wet rides and you can "recycle" them to another water-phobic person just entering the queue. They're also handy as an emergency stroller cover. Afternoon rain showers can roll up quickly in Orlando, even when the day dawns bright and sunny, and the ponchos are large enough to keep your stroller dry if you're taken by surprise. Keep ponchos in a Ziploc bag so even when they're wet, the rest of your bag will stay dry.

235.
Alternate Indoor and Outdoor Rides

Some areas of the parks have very little shade, making it necessary to seek refuge from the sun at regular intervals to avoid overheating. In Toy Story Land, ride Alien Swirling Saucers or Slinky Dog Dash first, then Toy Story Mania!, then the ride you haven't done yet, to give yourself a cooldown midway through your touring. If you make Slinky Dog Dash your Genie+ attraction, schedule it as your first or third ride in the land, making Toy Story Mania! your second ride for a longer break in air-conditioned comfort, then ride Alien Swirling Saucers as the alternate first or third ride. Animal Kingdom can be oppressively hot in summertime, so alternate outdoor rides with shows and rides with longer, indoor queues.

236.
Catch Holiday Fireworks a Day Early

Along with Christmas Day, two of the most heavily attended days at Magic Kingdom are the Fourth of July and New Year's Eve, in part because of the spectacular fireworks shows that end each of those holidays in high style. Magic Kingdom generally closes due to capacity on New Year's Eve, and it's shoulder to shoulder on Independence Day. Instead, do what savvy locals do and head into the park the day before. The special fireworks shows have their "dress rehearsal" on July 3 and December 30, respectively, and while Magic Kingdom will still be incredibly busy, you're far more likely to make it through the front gate without being turned away. Arrive early in the day, as the roadways will be at a standstill with last-minute arrivals.

237.
Navigate During a Parade

If you arrive at Magic Kingdom and discover a parade is in progress, making it difficult to get into the park through Town Square, head up the Main Street, U.S.A. Railroad Station stairs and take the train to Frontierland. Stuck at the back of the park during a parade and don't want to battle the crowds? Catch the train from Frontierland or Storybook Circus for a ride to the front of the park. There is a crossing point next to City Hall on Main Street, which Cast Members open at specific times during the parade for guests trying to exit the park, and it's the only safe place to cross. Don't be shy about dancing behind the banner at the end of the parade. Disney fans understand.

238.
Newbie Alert:
Theme Park Security Etiquette

Gone are the days of long bag-check lines, but you can still expedite the security process (especially when a boat, tram, or monorail has just unloaded). If you must bring a bag, be sure any items that will trigger the walk-through sensors (and result in a thorough bag search) are held out in front of you where Cast Members can see them. These items include (but are not limited to) umbrellas, portable chargers, and hard-sided glasses cases. Not sure what to remove? Ask a Cast Member. They want the process to go quickly too. Even if using the "No Bag" entry, the above items still need to be removed from pockets and held in front of you when passing through the sensors. Just visiting for a few hours? You can probably get away with your park admission, a credit card or cash, and your camera, none of which will trigger sensors.

239.
Avoid the Rough Side of the Water Parks

A day at a water park may be one of the best memories from your vacation, for its spontaneous, unstructured fun. Sure, you'll stand in a few lines, but there's a watery splashdown at the end and that counts for a lot from June through September. Amid all the enjoyment, there are three "rough" situations you'll want to avoid. Typhoon Lagoon's wave pool surface is textured; lift small children when the waves reach the shallow end to avoid skinned knees and elbows. Both water parks' sidewalks get hot, making water shoes a necessity. And then there's sand. Bring travel-sized baby powder to sprinkle on sandy skin for instant removal. Let your hair dry, dust with baby powder, brush, shake, shampoo, and those stubborn grains are gone.

Dress Up on Dapper Day

Why are all those Magic Kingdom visitors dressed as if it's the 1940s and they're stepping out in their Sunday finest? It's the fan event Dapper Day, which happens twice a year (spring and fall). Participants "dress to the nines" in any style they choose, from vintage to modern chic. The more detailed your outfit is, the better, so wear that flapper dress, boater hat and waistcoat, or 1950s prom dress, accessorize to the max, and be your most stylish self. It's all about looking and feeling fantastic. Not visiting during Dapper Day? Show up "dapper" anyway. The locals understand.

240.
Play Disney Parks App

Waiting in lines can be tedious, leading to cranky kids (and adults), but staring at individual smartphone screens isn't exactly a bonding experience. Instead, download the free Play Disney Parks app from Google Play or the Apple Store and enjoy multiplayer interactions that keep the whole family amused. The more you interact with the app, the more its various elements "come to life." Swipe right and left for items that appear just beyond the boundaries of the screen; watch for "Easter eggs" (little surprises) that pop up in the lands or queues; or listen to Disney music. There are games, challenges, trivia, and rewards and achievements for successful play. Most elements are triggered while you're in the parks, making it a special "only at Disney" experience.

241.
Translate Your Way Through World Showcase

Part of the fun when exploring EPCOT is the immersion in different cultures represented in the World Showcase pavilions. Mexico, Norway, China, Germany, Japan, Morocco, and France are beautifully detailed with signs and plaques, but how does a World Showcase traveler read the non-English elements if they don't speak the language? Download the free Google Translate app and use its camera translation mode to "read" text you see in each pavilion, such as the Mandarin writing over the false door between House of Good Fortune's real doors. Put the app into conversation mode and surprise Cast Members on Disney's Cultural Representative Program or Cultural Exchange Program with a conversation in their own language. When they respond in their native tongue, the app will translate for you.

242.
Do Theme Parks Without a Plan

With all the emphasis on planning, guests who like to "wing it" may feel the House of Mouse is no longer for them. But wait: You *can* visit without a plan. Arrive before park opening and ride the "biggies" without Genie+ or Individual Lightning Lane selections, use counter service instead of making dining reservations, and watch fireworks from less obvious places, such as Fantasyland in Magic Kingdom. Enter World Showcase at EPCOT as soon as it opens, and return to World Celebration, World Nature, and World Discovery after 5 p.m. Start at the back of the other parks and work your way forward. Then, stay for the second parade or other nighttime show, if there is one. It will be much easier to get the best viewing spots.

243.
Have an Allergy-Friendly Halloween Party

One of the highlights of the seasonal paid-for event Mickey's Not-So-Scary Halloween Party is the chance to go trick-or-treating at stations throughout the park. But what if an allergy or medical condition makes certain treats off-limits? When you pass through the designated entry for the event, inform the Cast Member handing out bags that there is an allergy in your group. You will be given a special bag that alerts Cast Members at the trick-or-treat stations, who will give you a token to redeem for allergy-friendly or non-food items. Then, stop at the first of two redemption locations you come to, enjoy a few treats, and redeem the rest of your tokens at the second location, usually in Town Square.

244.
Find the Quiet Spots in the Parks

The intense hubbub of the theme parks can wear on the nerves, especially after a few days of nonstop touring. Guests staying off-site and overstressed kids (or adults) in need of a quiet spot for a time-out aren't out of luck. The second floor of Columbia Harbour House in Magic Kingdom is practically deserted in the hours before and after lunch, and after dinner. Seek out the lakeside terrace between the United Kingdom and France pavilions in EPCOT's World Showcase. The short walkway next to Indiana Jones Adventure Outpost at Hollywood Studios is seldom used. In Animal Kingdom, enjoy the tiny riverside terrace behind Drinkwallah in Asia, or, outside of mealtimes, the pavilions behind Flame Tree Barbecue. You'll have near-solitude with a beautiful, relaxing view.

Magic Shots

PhotoPass photographers have a few tricks up their sleeves, and as they frame up your photo they may ask you to strike a specific pose. When you view your photo later, something—or someone—"magical" will appear in the shot. These digital inclusions are called Magic Shots, and they can be anything from Tinker Bell flying overhead to Stitch breaking through the pavement or the Orange Bird perched on your hand. Inclusions change periodically, and themed elements are added during seasonal events. If you're a dedicated planner, follow Disney PhotoPass Service on Facebook for all the current options. But it's more fun to be surprised!

245.
Ride Before Park Closing

You've done everything possible to ride a popular attraction, short of waiting in a three-hour line, but by the end of the day you've had no luck. Or, you loved an attraction so much you can't bear to leave the park without riding a second time. Maybe you just missed something, and you'll regret it if you don't fit it in before Mickey closes his parks down for the night. There is still hope. As long as you line up before the official park closing time has arrived, you will be allowed to ride. But do the Cast Members who are trying to shut the ride down a favor and don't enter the queue at the last second. This should only be a last-ditch option.

246.
Pro Alert: EPCOT Is Ideal for Toddlers

Wait…what? Everyone knows EPCOT is the "educational" park. It's for grownups, with next to nothing for the littlest guests to enjoy. Right? Wrong. When you make it your day-three park, it's ideal for giving toddlers a break from the sensory overload. There are even quiet sections where new walkers can be set free with little worry of being knocked over. Strip them down to the diaper and let them run through the splash fountains. Drop by every Kidcot Fun Stop in the park. Meet characters if they're into it, and take note: Out of twenty-two rides and attractions in EPCOT, there are only four that toddlers won't be able to try until they're older. That means a slower, low-key day, with minimal time apart.

247.
Little Visitors: Watch Out for Fireworks

Contrary to popular belief and the evidence that seems to be right in front of your eyes, Magic Kingdom's nighttime fireworks bursts are not launched from a location on or immediately behind Cinderella Castle. Although they appear to be directly over Fantasyland, the majority are launched from a site behind the park. However, some do originate in Fantasyland, and children who are frightened by the loud bursts won't want to be nearby when they go off. Avoid the buildings housing Peter Pan's Flight, Mickey's PhilharMagic, and The Many Adventures of Winnie the Pooh, and the rides inside. Alternative views are near Dumbo the Flying Elephant or Big Thunder Mountain Railroad.

248.
Silence the Fireworks

Still worried your kids aren't ready for fireworks? If you're staying at a Disney resort hotel, they can watch the fireworks in their pj's on the in-room Disney On Demand channel.

249.
Take Shelter with the Aliens

There isn't a great deal of cover in Toy Story Land, and that's a problem when the weather turns distinctly inclement. Like all outdoor roller coasters or rides, Slinky Dog Dash will close if there is lightning within ten miles of Walt Disney World, but Alien Swirling Saucers will remain open. Why? Because it's covered. However, there is one instance when the Aliens will stop what they're doing, and that's when an Orlando thunderstorm is so fierce that the rain comes in sideways. The good news is, the attraction will open to all guests in the area and act as a shelter from the rain. If the rain hammers down while you're exploring Andy's backyard, head to the attraction and wait out the storm.

250.
Genie+ and Ride Closures

You're happily trotting your way toward an attraction's boarding area, having scored a Genie+ return time, when you hear the dreaded announcement: The ride has gone down for an indeterminate length of time. So much for that Genie+ reservation, right? Wrong. Mickey wants you to be happy. If you've tapped through with your MagicBand or ticket, a new "any time" Genie+ will be added to your schedule and can be used for most rides, with a few exceptions. If your chosen ride opens again, it will show up as one of your My Disney Experience Genie+ selections. If not, enjoy something else without the wait. Not using Genie+? If you were near the front of the queue, ask the attraction's greeter for a paper return pass.

CHAPTER 6

ATTRACTIONS TO THE MAX

251.
Be "That Guy"

Some guests like to sit quietly at shows; others yearn to be in them. If you want to be "that guy" at Monsters, Inc. Laugh Floor, aim for the first six rows on the left side of the theater. You'll have the best chance of being chosen as the guy who gets picked on throughout the show. It also helps to be a bald, older man. If you're not, wear something wacky, be enthusiastic during the warm-up segment at the beginning of the show, and make yourself stand out from the crowd. It isn't a given you'll be chosen, but you will have a better-than-average chance. If you find yourself on the big screen and wish you weren't, dig deep and let your inner Disney out!

252.
Watch for Lucky Number 13

A wait time of thirteen minutes at Haunted Mansion in Magic Kingdom or at The Twilight Zone Tower of Terror in Disney's Hollywood Studios is just part of the magic. While the number thirteen may be unlucky for some, for you it's a gift. As you're passing by either of these attractions, or when you're checking the My Disney Experience app for wait times, if you see a posted wait time of thirteen minutes, make a beeline for the ride. This creepy nod to superstition means there is *no* wait for the attraction. It's all about the story at Disney, and this appropriately spooky insider insight means you'll be enjoying these Disney classics as a walk-on.

253.
Attend the Flag Retreat Ceremony

One of the most moving events at Magic Kingdom is the 5 p.m. (sometimes 5:30 p.m.) Flag Retreat ceremony in Town Square each day. Security personnel, the Color Guard, band members, and Disney's Dapper Dans gather for the lowering of the flag, and one member of the military attends as the guest of honor. For the best chance at being chosen, be in the Town Square area at park opening wearing something distinctly military, ideally a shirt and hat. Talk with Cast Members and make a comment about your appreciation for all Disney does for veterans. If you are redeeming military park admission, arrive at Will Call before park opening and mention your interest in the ceremony to the Cast Member who activates your ticket.

254.
Double Your Parade Photo Ops

Photo albums worldwide contain side-on shots of Magic Kingdom's Festival of Fantasy Parade, Boo-to-You Halloween Parade, or Once Upon A Christmastime Parade, but it's harder to get good shots that are directly head-on. Double your viewing angles by standing along the curb in front of Liberty Square Market, in the Hub facing straight down the walkway in front of The Hall of Presidents, or, the most magical of all, in Town Square's central park looking straight down Main Street. You'll get a view of the parade coming at you, and also a side view as it rounds each turn. The added benefit to Town Square is Cinderella Castle as your backdrop, and the relative ease of departure if you're leaving the park after the parade.

255.
Get Those Spontaneous
Meet-and-Greet Photos

Don't wait until everyone has posed before you take a picture at character meet-and-greets. Some of the best photos come from the spontaneous moments before everyone lines up for the shot, especially when it comes to youngsters. Have the person holding the camera stand to one side, halfway between the PhotoPass photographer and the character, if possible, and snap a shot of the kiddies running up to meet the character, Mom's teary eyes when the hugs start, and any antics the character pulls (Tigger, Chip and Dale, and Goofy are masters of hijinks). Don't overlook a close-up of excited family members' faces as they wait for their turn. They may turn out to be your sentimental favorites.

256.
Lessen the 4D Effects

Children (and a few adults!) experiencing an attraction with 4D effects can come away from it startled and unhappy, having been surprised by the water sprays, jets of air, or occasional unpleasant smells that add realism to the story being told. When you select a seat at a 4D attraction such as It's Tough to be a Bug!, Mickey's PhilharMagic, and Muppet*Vision 3D, look for small holes in the back of the seat in front of you. That's your clue that you'll be sprayed with mist or droplets of water, or an unnerving jet of air will shoot directly at you. If preparing your loved one in advance doesn't help, place something over the holes, or cover them with your hand.

257.
Go for a Less Intense
"It's Tough to be a Bug!"

It's Tough to be a Bug! is filled with sensory experiences designed to make you feel like you're being attacked by bugs. It has a massive scare factor for younger children, and even some adults are unnerved by the storyline's "surprises." With that in mind, and without giving away the fun for those who enjoy a good scare, place soft padding between timid guests and the backs of their chairs, and have young children sit cross-legged. Remind older kids and adults to straighten their legs so they're away from the bottom of the chair when the theater plunges into darkness, and again as the show ends and the voice-over tells "honorary bugs" to remain seated. Best hack with young children? Skip it until they're older! Take note, this show is scheduled for reimagining.

258.
Dine Your Way Into Frozen Ever After

Can't get a Genie+ time for Frozen Ever After? Willing to get up early and pay extra for the chance to ride without a wait? Try for an 8 a.m. booking at Akershus Royal Banquet Hall and you'll be in pole position when the attraction opens. Your goal is to be heading into the queue by 8:45 a.m. Bear in mind the possibility that park hours may change. If they do, and the park opens at 8 a.m., cancel your reservation at least twenty-four hours in advance. If you can't get an 8 a.m. booking, try for 9 a.m. or 9:15 a.m., show up at the front gate by 8 a.m., enter through the dining line, and ride the attraction before breakfast.

Smile for the Camera!

Anything goes when it comes to on-ride photo poses, as long as you're sitting down, your pose or gestures are safe and G-rated, and you're not disturbing others.

259. You're allowed to use small props, but be aware the rides will be at their most intense when the camera goes off (with the exception of Space Mountain) and it's hard not to hang on. If your Ray-Ban sunglasses or the Mickey plush you were posing with go flying, you won't see them again until the end of the day.

260. The drop on Tiana's Bayou Adventure is a fan favorite for wacky poses, including reading a newspaper or holding up signs. Coordinate a group photo with everyone wearing shower caps and using deodorant, or pretend you've all fallen asleep. The camera is below you as you plunge over the drop hill, so hold your pose for a few seconds.

261. Test Track's ride photo happens in the neon tunnel just before you crash into the wall at the end of the tunnel. Your car will pause at the start of the tunnel, then pick up speed. That's your cue to lament your impending doom.

262. The camera on The Twilight Zone Tower of Terror is exactly where you'd expect it to be: at the top of the tower, ready to flash just as you go into free fall. When the doors fly open you need to be in position, because you'll have a split second before you're plummeting downward again. As soon as you see a crack of daylight after your elevator rises to the top of the tower, feign an all-out scream!

263. Rock 'n' Roller Coaster Starring Aerosmith has a launch start, and the camera is located on the right-hand side as you're heading into the first tunnel. You'll be pressed back in your seat when the camera goes off, so simple poses, such as stern faces and Secret Service–style shades, work well here.

264. **Pretend an asteroid is about to strike or hold a park map as if you're reading it when you make the first turn on Space Mountain,** just after you exit the blue tunnel at the beginning of the ride. You'll have time to put props away as you climb the first lift hill, so this is a good one for more elaborate poses.

265. **Expedition Everest–Legend of the Forbidden Mountain's camera is located on the right-hand side,** immediately beyond the crest of the hill as you start your outdoor drop. Pretend you're fending off the Yeti you just passed…or make it look like he got you.

266. **Guardians of the Galaxy: Cosmic Rewind snaps your photo early on,** thank goodness, so you can hold on tight for the rest of the ride. The first time your Starjumper rotates and launches you backward, get ready. At the second rotation, strike that pose!

267. **The photo op for TRON Lightcycle/Run is unique in two ways:** It takes both still photos and video AND its cameras are positioned on both sides so you'll be the star of the show no matter which cycle you choose. Now's your chance for some movement in your pose!

268. **The more over-the-top dramatic you are, the better your photos will be, so go for it!** You'll be glad you did when you return home and relive the memories.

269.
Watch Out for Inflated Wait Times

During the last hour of the day you may notice ride wait times going up, but that doesn't necessarily mean there is actually a long wait at the attraction. If the Standby display at a ride you'd like to try shows a long wait time, but you can't see the end of the line, start walking the queue. Some attractions will inflate their wait times as they prepare to close for the day, to discourage guests from queuing up, and it's a pretty effective trick, which could be good news for those who dare to ignore it. That forty-five-minute posted time could turn out to be more like ten or fifteen minutes.

270.
Score the Coveted Middle Seats

It's true: The center of the theater usually gives you the clearest view of 3D shows. It's also true you'll earn the justified ire of guests and Cast Members alike if you plop down in the middle of the row and refuse to fill in remaining seats. While the competitive urge to be first kicks in when you're in a big crowd, ignoring it in this situation will land you in the middle seat without all the drama. When you enter the theater, decide which few rows you would like to sit in, and allow other guests to file past you until one of your chosen rows is half full. Then, head in and score the perfect view without angry neighbors glaring at you throughout the show.

271.
Beat the Deleted Photos

If you were planning to purchase your ride photo only to discover it was ruined by someone making a gesture or doing something on Disney's "naughty" list, and therefore, the photo was "filtered out" (Disney-speak for deleting the photo immediately), mention the lost photo to a Cast Member at the attraction's photo counter and they will make sure you're escorted to the front of the queue so you can ride again without waiting. If you have purchased Memory Maker or are an Annual Passholder with the Memory Maker add-on, and the photo is important to you, be sure to look for it on the monitor in the photo processing room after you exit the attraction rather than assuming the photo went straight onto your account.

272.
Go Footless Soarin'

When the Cast Members at Soarin' Around the World direct you to the holding area's three sections, ask if you can have the first-row seating and you'll have a view of the screen that doesn't include the dangling feet of the people above you. Rows A-1, B-1, and C-1 swing into the highest position on the ride structure, which means there will be no one above you. Row 2 will be in the middle and Row 3 will be closest to the ground. You may be required to wait for the next show if Row 1 is already full, but you will just be held to one side until previous riders enter the theater, and you won't have to line up again.

273.
Adjust TRON's Thrill Factor

Walt Disney World's TRON Lightcycle/Run coaster features cycle-style seating which positions riders "face first." If you want to maximize the visual thrill-factor, ask for the first row and scream your way through the neon void in front of you. If you want to be whipped around a bit more, go for the back row, which has greater torque as you plummet down each descent.

Take the "Chicken Exit"

Thrill rides aren't for everyone, but sometimes you don't want to split your group up or be the lone family member sitting on a curb outside the attraction. Every thrill ride at Disney includes an exit for guests who can't ride the attraction, or choose not to, but still want to walk through the queue with their group. This exit is located at or near the ride's boarding area. Simply tell the loading Cast Member you're not riding and they'll direct you to the exit. Take note: The non-rider exit for The Twilight Zone Tower of Terror involves an actual elevator.

274.
Ride TRON Lightcycle/Run in Comfort

If TRON's cycle seats don't work for you (there's a test seat at the queue entrance), some trains have a regular coaster car at the back, which you can request when you get to the front of the queue. Just ask the Cast Member before boarding, and they'll put you on "hold" until the right train arrives.

275.
Experience the Full
Cosmic Rewind Playlist

Guardians of the Galaxy: Cosmic Rewind features six different songs from Star-Lord's awesome playlist: "September" by Earth, Wind & Fire; "Disco Inferno" by The Trammps; "Conga" by Gloria Estefan; "Everybody Wants to Rule the World" by Tears for Fears; "I Ran" by A Flock of Seagulls; and "One Way or Another" by Blondie. You never know which soundtrack you're going to get, so it's worth re-riding to potentially hear a new one. The experience "feels" a little bit different depending on which music is playing.

276.
View the American Adventure Up Close

Although the best seat in the house is usually in the middle of the theater, that isn't necessarily the case at The American Adventure. Front-row seats, especially in the center, offer a terrific view of some of the finer details, including the glowing ash at the end of Mark Twain's cigar and the clever mechanics Disney Imagineers use to make the Audio-Animatronic Benjamin Franklin walk up the stairs. There are no bad seats in the theater, and the broader view afforded by middle and rear seats is worth seeking out, especially for first-timers, but if you find yourself in the first ten rows, don't worry. You'll see certain elements clearly that will be less noticeable from farther back.

277.
Visit Fantasyland First

Yes, it's okay if you're over the age of ten and you still love Pooh Bear and Tigger, Peter Pan, Dumbo, and that most classic of Disney experiences, singing and dancing children from around the world. If the Fantasyland attractions are more important to you than the thrill rides, arrive for park opening and make Peter Pan's Flight, The Many Adventures of Winnie the Pooh, and "it's a small world" your first rides of the day, in that order. Wait times will increase quickly, so if you don't arrive in time for shorter queues, save Fantasyland for the last hour or two of the day, when most of the happy, tired children and their battle-weary parents have returned to their resorts for the night.

278.
Book Extra Terror on the Tower

Along with a spooky storyline and terrifying drop sequence, The Twilight Zone Tower of Terror affords a fantastic view of the park when your elevator reaches the top of the Tower and the doors fly open. For the best view of this spectacle—which is even more awesome at night—request position one or position two when the Cast Member assigns rows before you board your elevator. That will put you right in the front row, for an extra dose of both "Wow!" and "Yikes!" If you prefer not to see how high up you are, ask for position five or position six and you'll be seated at the back of the elevator. The semi-adventurous rows are positions three and four, right in the middle.

Use PhotoPass

PhotoPass is a photography service in Disney's theme parks, Disney Springs, and certain dining locations. All guests may use it, and there is no obligation to purchase the photos. A PhotoPass photographer takes one or more digital photos of you or your group, then scans your MagicBand or admission ticket linked to your My Disney Experience account or provides you with a free PhotoPass card, which can be used throughout your vacation. Within thirty days of returning home, select the photos you like best, decorate with Disney borders if you wish, then purchase your selections for printing or sharing.

The Famed "Disney Walls"

Disney fans have made certain foods, drinks, and attractions into "cult classics," and they've done the same with specific walls within the theme parks. Several locations offer the best generic backdrops for your social media photos, with their bold colors and geometric shapes. You just need to know where to find them.

279. Take the walkway that links Tomorrowland Terrace and Tomorrowland, and look to your right. Magic Kingdom's Purple Wall, the one that started it all, is found on the Monsters, Inc. building between Tomorrowland Terrace and Tomorrowland.

280. EPCOT's Toothpaste Wall is found to the left of the entry door for Coral Reef Restaurant at The Seas with Nemo & Friends; the Bubblegum Wall, in bright raspberry, pink, and blue, is located outside both exits at Spaceship Earth. The tricolored Blueberry Wall is right there too.

281. Hollywood Studios has a fun Popsicle Stick Wall at the exit for Toy Story Mania! Walk along the first bend in the exit queue, after the Barrel of Monkeys, and the Popsicle Stick Wall will be on your left.

282. Animal Kingdom's gorgeous Moss Wall is located in Pandora–The World of Avatar, directly across from the entry into Satu'li Canteen and to your right if you're exiting Windtraders. There are a few more moss-covered walls in Pandora, each with its own "personality."

283. There are several other walls that have made their way up the social media ladder too. Look for the bold floral designs at the Tangled restrooms between Fantasyland and Liberty Square, and the bright blue wall around the corner from the exit for Buzz Lightyear's Space Ranger

Spin in Magic Kingdom; the Mosaic Walls that lead up to The Land pavilion's entrance in EPCOT; the colorful Building Block Wall at the restroom water fountains in Toy Story Land, and the Checkers Wall directly across from the Popsicle Stick Wall at Hollywood Studios; and the wall that reads "You Are Most Beautiful" at Africa's Harambe Market in Animal Kingdom.

284. **Many of the walls have their own hashtag (for example, #PurpleWall and #MossWall), so be sure to post your efforts on Instagram.** And remember: Every one of these walls became a social media star because of enthusiastic Disney fans just like you, so don't be afraid to keep your eyes open for other Instagram-worthy walls. You may just start a trend!

285.
Keep Your Feet Dry on Kali River Rapids

You will not be allowed to remove your shoes when riding Kali River Rapids, but that silver bar encircling the storage bin in the middle of the raft is there for a reason. Put your feet on it before your raft launches, and keep them there. You'll have a better-than-average chance they'll stay relatively dry. Not taking any chances? Once you're seated, grab two of those jumbo Ziploc bags you're carrying in your backpack and two of your rubber bands, quickly put the bags over your shoes (while they're still on your feet), cinch the tops shut with the rubber bands, and arrive at the unloading platform with dry feet. Be sure to remove the bags before you stand up!

286.
Make a Quick Change to
Avoid Sopping-Wet Shoes

Carry inexpensive rubber flip-flops in your backpack, and before queuing for a wet ride, switch out shoes and socks for the waterproof footwear and switch back when the ride is over (this is also a good shoe-saver during Orlando's "unexpected" rain showers).

287.
Get the Best Fireworks View

When is an up-front view not worth having? When you're watching the Happily Ever After nighttime fireworks at Magic Kingdom. Instead of scrambling for a spot as close to the castle as possible, leave that rookie mistake to those who aren't in the know and stake out a spot at least as far back as the *Partners* statue of Walt Disney and Mickey Mouse. Make sure there are no trees blocking your view of the sky surrounding the top of Cinderella Castle. The best view in the park is from the second floor of the Main Street, U.S.A. Railroad Station, but you'll have to arrive at least an hour in advance, and you need to be standing right along the front railing to get maximum benefit.

288.
Choose a "Moving Buddy"

Alien Swirling Saucers in Toy Story Land at Hollywood Studios has a special requirement: You need to know who your "moving buddy" will be in advance of boarding your rocket ship. In the original Toy Story movie, Woody holds a meeting informing the toys they'll need a moving buddy for Andy's impending move to a new home, so that no toy is left behind. You should do the same while you're in the queue getting ready for your swirl around the universe. Each rocket ship can fit two children and one adult, or two adults, so pair up with your "moving buddy" before you reach the loading area. A family of four (or three adults) won't fit into one spaceship, so plan accordingly.

289.
Tamest Rows on Slinky Dog Dash

The front seats on most Disney roller coasters are desirable for guests who like a tamer version of the ride, and while that recommendation does hold true for Slinky Dog Dash in Toy Story Land at Hollywood Studios, there is one little niggle that makes the front seats somewhat less desirable: that enormous Slinky Dog head. Although the drops and turns feel slightly less intense in the two front seats, you won't be able to see the track ahead of you so you'll miss some of the fun. Instead, request row three, four, or five, if possible. Your ride will still feel less dynamic, but you'll be able to anticipate each element of the coaster and enjoy all the scenery.

Don't Rely On the Wait Times

When is fifty minutes not really fifty minutes? When it's a posted wait time at a theme park attraction, and there are several reasons why waits may be longer or shorter than stated. Rides may stop temporarily to assist guests with mobility issues; additional ride vehicles may have been transitioned in; or the time it takes for a random guest's MagicBand to go from the entry point for the queue to the boarding area hasn't been "sampled" and entered recently. Add and subtract ten to fifteen minutes to the estimate and line up—or not—based on those numbers.

290.
Experience the Full Queue

By all means, use Genie+, Individual Lightning Lane selections, and Single Rider lines to their very best advantage, but if time permits, there are some attractions with such beautifully themed queues it would be a shame to miss them. After you've ridden once, try to fit in a Standby ride on the following: Haunted Mansion, Peter Pan's Flight, and The Many Adventures of Winnie the Pooh at Magic Kingdom; Guardians of the Galaxy: Cosmic Rewind at EPCOT; Star Tours–The Adventures Continue, Star Wars: Galaxy's Edge attractions, and The Twilight Zone Tower of Terror at Hollywood Studios; and Avatar Flight of Passage, Kali River Rapids, and Expedition Everest–Legend of the Forbidden Mountain at Animal Kingdom. Early morning and late night are usually best for shorter waits.

291.
Snag the Best Attraction Seats

Just like the shows, some rides are best experienced from specific seats. For the overall view, the best seats on Kilimanjaro Safaris are the back rows. Seat the photographer in your group on the left-hand side. The animals will be on both sides, but most settings are situated on the left. While you can get wet on any Tiana's Bayou Adventure seat, the first two rows are most vulnerable; back row, left-hand side is driest. Most Disney roller coasters are less intense in the front row, and more intense in the back, including TRON Lightcycle/Run at Magic Kingdom. All seats on Avatar Flight of Passage are pretty spectacular, but the middle seats have slightly clearer graphics than the end seats.

292.
Haunted Mansion Squeeze

Haunted Mansion is one of Disney's classic attractions, and it's been a fan favorite since opening day. Its lasting popularity also means the indoor preshow and queue, built in 1971, were designed with much smaller crowds in mind. When you enter the preshow "stretch room," aim for a spot under the portrait of the woman holding a pink parasol. The door to the queue is located on that side of the room. Once you exit, the wide hallway you enter will narrow down to single file. Make a beeline for the left side of the hallway as soon as you leave the stretch room, especially if you're not among the first to exit, and you won't get caught in the squeeze as guests enter the narrow queue.

293.
Get the Inside Scoop on Challenging Attractions with Youngsters

It can be tough being a small fry when it comes to challenging attractions. If your group's competitive spirit comes out on Buzz Lightyear's Space Ranger Spin or Toy Story Mania!, don't worry. Buzz's smallest space rangers will score 1,300 points just by clicking the trigger, and Toy Story Mania! was designed so that riders of all skill levels feel successful, even if they aren't gamers (that means grandmas and grandpas who roll "old school" too!). Slinky Dog Dash is another ride youngsters may find intimidating, but it was created as an "aspirational" roller coaster so that kids who view it as a major thrill ride will come away from the experience feeling proud they met the challenge.

294.
Don't Miss the Best Themed Standby Queues

If you can get the Genie+ time or Individual Lightning Lane, get the Genie+ time or Individual Lightning Lane; but six attractions' Standby queues are so detailed it isn't a tragedy if you have to walk through them. Avatar Flight of Passage is among the most immersive in Walt Disney World. Look for evidence that reveals the Resources Development Administration and the Na'vi have each left their mark, as well as Imagineer and designer "signatures" such as birth dates and handprints. Star Tours and the two attractions in Star Wars: Galaxy's Edge are filled with references from the Star Wars movies, and the baggage scanner in the Star Tours queue is hilarious. Guardians of the Galaxy: Cosmic Rewind features references to the movies, and to EPCOT's history, while Expedition Everest–Legend of the Forbidden Mountain's queue builds the excitement with real and "imagined" artifacts, plus photographs from the actual research expeditions Disney Imagineers took when designing the attraction.

Find the Attractions That Don't Need Genie+

Some attractions that offer Genie+ never have wait times long enough to justify using your precious choices. Instead, enjoy these at midday, when it's hot and the lines are long: Mickey's PhilharMagic, "it's a small world," and Monster's, Inc. Laugh Floor at Magic Kingdom; Journey Into Imagination with Figment and the Disney & Pixar Short Film Festival at EPCOT; A Frozen Sing-Along Celebration, Indiana Jones Epic Stunt Spectacular!, Muppet*Vision 3D, Disney Junior, and Beauty and the Beast–Live on Stage at Hollywood Studios; and the shows It's Tough to be a Bug! and Feathered Friends in Flight! at Animal Kingdom.

295.
Rides You Must Do Twice

Most attractions have good repeat value, meaning they're enjoyable no matter how many times you ride them. Four attractions stand out for their ability to feel like a new ride, and you'll miss out if you don't try them at least twice. The animals you'll see during Kilimanjaro Safaris will vary depending on the time of day, as some animals are more active in the morning while others prefer the midday heat, and the after-dark experience is completely different than a daytime ride. The Twilight Zone Tower of Terror works on a random drop sequence, and you never know what you'll get. With special "extras," Star Tours–The Adventures Continue has nearly 300 variations, so it's possible to ride several times and not have the same experience twice, while Star Wars: Rise of the Resistance features two versions, each with distinct as well as overlapping scenes.

296.
Beat the Lines at Frozen Ever After During EPCOT's Fireworks

The line for Frozen Ever After remained prohibitive and you couldn't get a Genie+ time. You're not willing to pay the no-show cancellation fee for an unused booking at Akershus Royal Banquet Hall, just to be first in the Standby queue, and you're not willing to get up before the birds for a five-minute ride, no matter how good it is. There is one final possibility: Line up shortly before EPCOT's nightly fireworks spectacular begins. Standby will drop by roughly twenty minutes right before the show, and as long as you're in line, you'll get in. The queue will close just before the fireworks begin, so if you arrive once it starts you'll be too late.

297.
Be the Rebel Spy

Part of the storyline of Star Tours–The Adventures Continue involves a subplot: Your transport is harboring a rebel spy. There are no guarantees, but you can maximize your chances if you'd like to be chosen. It's all down to the operator, but kids and people in big groups stand a good chance. The row you're seated in doesn't matter, so store your gear and buckle up as fast as you can. Then, let your face do the rest. Assume a stern look or a silly face, and make sure you're facing forward. The rebel spy doesn't wear 3D glasses, so leave them off. If you're wearing a hat, remove it. In short, try to look like you might really *be* a rebel spy.

298.
For the Best Animal Sightings, Take an Afternoon Safari

Animal Kingdom is the most real-life of all the Disney parks, and a ride on Kilimanjaro Safaris is close to the genuine safari experience in Africa. To see the animals at their most active, the best strategy is to book an early Genie+ time, especially in summer when the animals seek refuge from the afternoon heat. If Genie+ bookings for the park's thrill rides are more important to you than a trundle along the savanna, you're not out of luck. Some of the animals you'll see on your safari will return to their nighttime enclosures around 3 p.m., and they become more active as their "offstage" hour approaches. If you don't ride in the morning, plan for a 2:30 p.m. or 2:45 p.m. ride instead.

299.
Take In Two Shows in One Night

You've got one day at Hollywood Studios and you want to watch Fantasmic! and Wonderful World of Animation. If you're visiting when Fantasmic! has two showings, you're in luck. Head to the early showing of Fantasmic! and choose a row on the far right-hand side, close to the back of the theater. You'll have the quickest exit at the end of the show. For an unobstructed view of Wonderful World of Animation, stake out a spot in the middle of Hollywood Boulevard, facing the center of the Chinese Theater, forward of the projection towers but not too close to the theater. Bring a towel along to "mark your territory," as guests tend to sit while waiting, then stand during the show.

CHAPTER 7

HOME AWAY FROM HOME

300.
Modify Your Reservation

You've done your homework, you've found the best deal possible on a Disney resort, but sure enough, once you've paid your deposit, a slew of special offers pops up. Fear not. Simply call Reservations at 407-939-4357 and request a reservation modification, bearing in mind you may need a code to receive some discounts. Always check Disney's "Special Offers" page online before booking, but if a discount crops up that you're able to use, call and the agent will update your reservation. Discounts cannot be applied online, and they will not be applied to your reservation automatically. You have to ask for them. Be aware, some discounts are offered in limited numbers, so you may have to be quick about making your request.

301.
Thank the Mousekeepers

Mousekeepers, Disney's version of housekeepers, are the people who clean your room, fluff your pillows, ensure you have all the towels you need, and, when they are able, make sure there is a bit of Disney magic in store when you return to your room after a long day. Instead of leaving a few dollars on a nightstand or pillow, decorate enough envelopes for each night of your stay and slip their tip inside. Personalized envelopes are easier for Mousekeeping to identify and a thoughtful touch as they go about their duties. Be sure to leave a tip each night rather than on the last day of your vacation, as more than one Mousekeeper may attend to you over the course of your stay. Full Mousekeeping service may not be offered every day in some resort hotels, but you can call them if you need something.

302.
Rent DVC Points

Disney calls the Disney Vacation Club (DVC) its "best kept secret," but happily for guests seeking lots of luxury on a moderate budget, the popularity of this timeshare accommodation isn't a secret at all. Owners purchase "points," which are used to book reservations at DVC resorts, and while you may not be ready to commit to a contract, nonmembers can stay in a DVC property by renting from an owner who isn't using their points during any given year. There are several websites that "rent" DVC points, including David's Vacation Club Rentals, www.dvcrequest.com, and DVC Rental Store, https://dvcrentalstore.com. Confirm terms, request your travel dates, pay the points rental, and a reservation will be made in your name. Then, enjoy all the perks of an on-site stay!

303.
Save Big with Resort Refillable Mugs

Plan a rest day from the parks and go "resort hopping," or visit the resorts for dining and resort-based activities. Purchase a refillable mug at the first resort you visit and you can refill it with soft drinks, tea, coffee, or hot chocolate for the duration of your vacation. You can't use it for drink refills at the theme parks, but you can bring it along and fill it with water at the drinking fountains. Take note: All Disney refillable mugs have an RFID bar code that expires at the end of your trip, and they become souvenirs at that point. You're welcome to bring them along during future vacations, but you won't be able to refill them for free.

304.
Hack Some Instant Blackout Shades

You've had a long day in the bright sunshine, going nonstop in the parks, and the only thing you can think of is eight blissful hours of uninterrupted sleep. If you return to your hotel and discover you've been saddled with those annoying curtains that don't overlap when you close them, which means you're going to get an eyeful of the rising sun at 6 a.m., there is still hope for a 9 a.m. wake-up time. Use binder clips to clip the curtains shut. What if you didn't bring any? Grab one or two of the hangers with clips on them from your closet, and clip the curtains together. Hello darkness, my new friend!

305.
Get a Room Upgrade

When booking your Walt Disney World hotel room directly through Disney's Reservations, ask if there are any upgrades once you've settled on a date and a resort, and have indicated you want to book the reservation. If you are booking a Value resort, you may be offered an upgrade to a Moderate; if booking a Moderate, you may be offered an upgrade to a Deluxe. There will be an extra per-night charge, but if the upgrade is available and the Disney booking agent is accommodating, the extra charge will be less than the rack rate for the upgraded room. Failing that, you might get an upgrade to a better room view at the resort you book if you ask nicely about availability at check-in.

306.
Enjoy Ice-Cold Water for Hours

One of the great joys of summertime vacations comes from a bottle. A water bottle, that is. It's common knowledge that chilling water overnight pays big dividends the next day, but the effect only lasts so long when the temperature soars into the nineties. Adding ice helps, but you'll only have an hour or so before your water goes warm. If your accommodation has a refrigerator with a freezer, fill your water bottle two-thirds full, lay it on its side, and freeze it overnight. Then, fill it with water in the morning and you'll have ice-cold water for several hours. Take note: Condensation can leach the color out of insulated fabric bottle holders on a lanyard, so avoid prolonged contact with your clothing.

307.
Mail Packages to Disney's Resorts

Whether you want to save space and weight in your luggage, avoid a grocery stop after a late arrival, or ship Christmas, birthday, or other celebratory gifts to your Disney resort so that they stay top secret, front desk Cast Members are happy to hold your packages until you arrive. Follow this addressing formula exactly, include the word "guest" on the front of the package, agree to a modest handling fee, and your delivery will find you:

- **Guest name:** (name of the person who will collect the package)
- **C/O:** (add your resort name after C/O)
- **Hold for guest arriving on:** (add your arrival date here)
- **Reservation number:** (add your Disney resort reservation number)
- **Resort address:** (complete labeling with your resort's full address)

Go Solo at Disney; Best Trip Ever!

You're surrounded by the cheerful laughter of children, the adoring gazes of honeymooners wearing bride-and-groom Mickey ears, and joyful families bonding in the most magical destination on Earth. Who's the happiest person in the park? You. Because you're visiting Walt Disney World as a solo traveler, and there is nothing more freeing than that.

308. The number one reason visiting Disney on your own is such a fantastic experience is you get to call all the shots. Eat what and when you want, sleep when you're ready, and never spend one moment compromising. It's all about you, so make the most of your "single" status.

309. Use the Single Rider queue at attractions that offer it, because during this trip, you're special. If you want to meet your seatmates, ask if they've "ridden this one before." If you're reveling in your solitude so much you're unwilling to share a seat with a stranger, use the Standby queue and ask the Cast Member loading the ride if you can have the row to yourself. If they can, they'll make it happen.

310. By using Single Rider and visiting only the rides and attractions that appeal to you, you'll have more free time than you would if you were traveling with a group. Make the most of it by searching for "hidden Mickeys," the three-circle representations of Mickey Mouse's head and ears, as you walk around the parks and take in the rides.

311. Delve deep into the backstories of the attractions and the fabulous hidden secrets in the parks with The Hidden Magic of Walt Disney World book series. Wandering around with your book in hand searching for the little things that make the parks special is a great way to connect with other visitors in short but enjoyable conversations that won't impinge on your laid-back non-schedule.

312. **Singles don't have to give up experiences that usually require more than one person.** Love to meet the characters? Hand your phone to the PhotoPass photographers and they'll take your photo for free. It's not an imposition; they're happy to make your interaction special. Want a photo anywhere else in the parks? Just ask the nearest Cast Member, as long as she or he isn't busy with another task.

313. **Sign up for a behind-the-scenes tour if you'd like bonding time with other Disney fans,** enjoy the benefits of a walk-up dining reservation for one, wander through the minor exhibits in EPCOT, or ride Tiana's Bayou Adventure ten times in a row. And eat ice cream for breakfast.

314. **If you're craving raucous, communal fun at the end of the day,** make Jellyrolls dueling piano bar at Disney's BoardWalk Inn your grand finale, or head to Port Orleans for the wacky Yehaa Bob Jackson at River Roost Lounge. Yehaa Bob's show is free. Then, the next time you visit Walt Disney World with family or friends, watch for the solo travelers and smile at your shared bond of having experienced the parks like Pinocchio: with no strings attached.

315.
Create a Makeshift Kitchen

Orlando mornings are decidedly chilly in winter, and you may want more than a cold bowl of cereal in your room to get your day off on the right foot. For those grab-and-go mornings, or nights when you can't face another heavy meal, bring along some "instant" foods and press your in-room coffee maker, iron, and ironing board into service. Stir up a steaming mug of oatmeal, ramen, or soup-in-a-cup using hot water from your coffee maker. Wrap bread and cheese in aluminum foil and put your iron to work for grilled cheese sandwiches. Set up the ironing board at the edge of the bed for an impromptu table, and you've got a mini kitchen serving up hot food for just a few dollars.

Early Theme Park Entry and Extended Evening Hours

Guests staying at any Disney resort are entitled to use Early Theme Park Entry each day, which allows them to enter a specified theme park thirty minutes before regular park opening, while those staying in one of Disney's Deluxe Resorts, a Deluxe Villa, or select partner hotels may remain in a specified park for two additional hours after regular park closing during Extended Evening Hours. These "bonus" hours and corresponding parks are chosen by Disney, and the schedule specific to your vacation dates will be listed in your My Disney Experience app at check-in, or you can view them in advance under "Park Hours" on the www.disneyworld .disney.go.com website.

316.
Ask for an Upgrade

Slipping the front desk attendants an Andrew Jackson ($20) might work if you're angling for a room upgrade in New York, but it won't work at a Disney resort. Cast Members won't take it, and you don't need bribery to get something special. If it's possible to make your smile a little brighter, Cast Members can often make that happen. Are you celebrating something special that isn't notated on your reservation? Is this your first time visiting Walt Disney World? Mention it to the Cast Member at check-in. If you're feeling particularly bold, ask if there are any little perks available. There is no guarantee, but politeness goes a long way, and if magic can happen there's a good chance it will.

317.
Give Yourself an Upgrade

Staying in a basic hotel room doesn't mean you have to do without niceties. You won't be offered a pillow menu, but you can ask for extra towels. If you find one pillow is too squishy but two are too high, insert dry, folded towels into the pillowcase until you get just the right firmness. You are unlikely to find a docking station in a standard room, so pop your phone into a coffee mug or bathroom glass for an instant amplifier, not only for your playlist but for a louder alarm for those early Genie+ reservations or dining times. Dank smell from Florida's humidity? Use your binder clips to attach an unused coffee packet to the air-conditioning unit.

318.
Go On an Adults' Night Out

Everyone feels like a kid during their day in a theme park, but after twelve hours of pixie dust you might be craving something a bit more grown-up by evening-time. You could pay a cover charge for Jellyrolls at Disney's BoardWalk Inn, but all guests are welcome to enjoy the free live entertainment with an intimate atmosphere at various resorts and Disney Springs. Among the best are the live pianist's mellow tunes at the Grand Floridian Resort; live jazz at Scat Cat's Club in Port Orleans–French Quarter; and The Front Porch at Disney Springs West Side's House of Blues. Want a far more rollicking evening? Belly up to the bar at Raglan Road for live Irish music late into the night.

319.
Get Some Tea Bag Sunburn Relief

In spite of your best efforts with the sunblock, you've got a nasty burn on the skin you couldn't quite reach. If you don't have hemorrhoid cream or aloe vera (ideally cooling in your mini fridge for maximum "Ahhhhhhhh…"), grab two tea bags from your coffee station condiments, fill your ice bucket or the bathroom sink with several inches of water, and steep the tea bags in it until the water turns a deep, dark brown. Then, soak a washcloth in the tea water, wring it out just until it's not dripping wet, and drape it over your suffering lobster skin. Be sure to rinse the washcloth well as soon as you're done or the tea stain will remain.

320.
Accommodate Large Parties

Most Disney resort rooms accommodate four to five guests. When traveling with a group larger than five, you do have choices if you all want to stay in the same place. Disney's All-Star Music and Art of Animation resorts have six-guest suites, while cabins at Fort Wilderness also sleep six. Sleep eight in most two-bedroom villas, or up to nine in a two-bedroom villa at Old Key West, Bay Lake Tower, Grand Floridian, or Kidani Village, or the Saratoga Springs Treehouse Villas, BoardWalk Lock-Off Villas, or Polynesian Villas & Bungalows. Up to twelve will fit in Wilderness Lodge's Copper Creek three-bedroom Grand Villa. Always compare single-accommodation pricing against the cost of two or more rooms, especially at discounted rates.

Bounceback Offers

That "Welcome" booklet in your Disney resort room is filled with useful tidbits, and among the most magical are the "bounceback" offers. As an incentive for booking your next vacation early, Disney often features limited-time, limited-availability discounts, including room-only discounts and free Disney Dining Plans or Dining Plan upgrades. You can also call extension 8844 on your resort phone to ask what's available. Then, pay a deposit and your next vacation is booked before your current trip is over. If plans change, you can cancel within thirty days or modify to new dates if the discount still applies.

321.
Decorate Your Room

To set the seasonal mood when you're away from friends and extended family over Christmas or Halloween, bring along (or purchase upon arrival) strings of orange lights and other Halloween decorations in October, or Christmas lights, garland, a tabletop tree, and stockings at Christmas, and decorate your hotel room. Before leaving Disney, turn your used decorations into a heartwarming, special gift. Starting in mid-December, several locations around Orlando accept donations of battery-operated Christmas lights and other holiday decorations, to aid The Greyson Project in brightening up rooms for children staying in local hospitals over Christmas. Check the website www.thegreysonproject.org for drop-off points.

322.
Continue Your Fitness Routine

Your normal fitness routine includes an early morning jog, and although you'll be doing a lot of walking, you want to keep that healthy habit going. Perhaps you just enjoy an evening stroll. You're in luck. There are several walkways at the Disney resorts that fit the bill. Try the boardwalk connecting the Yacht and Beach Clubs, the BoardWalk Inn, and the Swan and Dolphin Resorts, with paths ranging from .08 to four miles. Fort Wilderness has a two-and-a-half-mile walkway, with a three-quarter-mile extension leading to Wilderness Lodge; a one-mile path connects the Polynesian Village and Grand Floridian resorts; and the Port Orleans twin resorts link via a 1.7-mile walkway. Saratoga Springs, Old Key West, the Contemporary, All-Star, and Caribbean Beach resorts each have walking paths.

323.
Pro Alert: Do Online Check-In

Are you a longtime, room-only visitor without a Disney Dining Plan? Why start your vacation with a tedious wait at check-in? Up to sixty days prior to arrival, access My Reservations on My Disney Experience for online check-in. Provide your credit card information and contact details, choose a PIN number, add your estimated arrival time, and have paid-for MagicBands sent to your home. Head to a park or the pool when you arrive and you'll get a text or email with your room number when it's ready. Then, bypass the front desk and head straight to your room. Anyone can use online check-in, but first-timers shouldn't miss the thrill of hearing "Welcome home" at the front desk.

324.
Hack a Hair Dryer Quick Fix

You got caught in a surprise rainstorm and ended up with wet socks. Put your hotel room hair dryer to work by placing each sock over the blower end and drying them from the inside out. Can't squeeze one more drop out of your toothpaste tube? Warm it with the hair dryer and you'll have enough for a final brushing before you head to the store for another tube. Scraped your knee in the wave pool at Typhoon Lagoon? Avoid the "ouch" from the adhesive bandage by warming it with the hair dryer first. Can't remove the price tag from that cool souvenir you just purchased? Warm it with the hair dryer and it'll pull right off, with no sticky residue.

Christmas at Disney

The week between Christmas and the New Year is unquestionably the busiest time of the year at Walt Disney World, so much so that Magic Kingdom closes due to capacity either temporarily or all day on Christmas Day and New Year's Eve, with crowds nearly as large on Christmas Eve.

Guests entering the parks with the intention of soaking up the atmosphere rather than rushing from ride to ride are rewarded with gorgeous decorations throughout Magic Kingdom, culminating in the jaw-dropping beauty of Cinderella Castle's icy overlay at night; the brilliant International Festival of the Holidays and enchanting Holiday Storytellers in World Showcase, plus the moving Candlelight Processional retelling of the Nativity story at EPCOT; and Sunset Seasons Greetings and nighttime Jingle Bell, Jingle BAM! fireworks show at Hollywood Studios. You'll find "Florida snow," Santa makes appearances, Christmas trees abound, and there are special foods, drinks, and parties to round out the joyous season.

With all the happy hubbub in the parks, the resorts are sometimes overlooked, but they offer the perfect retreat from the holiday madness. A day spent enjoying their seasonal elements will make you forget the crowds and the fact that it's eighty degrees outside with no "real" snow. All of the Disney resorts decorate for Christmas, but there are a few standouts that capture the Yuletide spirit best.

325. Disney's Wilderness Lodge has everything a rustic cabin in the woods should have at Christmastime, and guests who live in places that really know what winter feels like will be utterly at home here. A massive Christmas tree in the lobby makes a nostalgic backdrop, and cozy seats around the crackling fire are the quintessential setting when a blizzard blows in. Florida won't have one, but you'll almost be convinced it could.

326. Guests seeking a Victorian experience will find it at the Grand Floridian Resort. From the sixteen-foot-high gingerbread house and enormous Christmas tree in the lobby, to wreaths and garland dripping in elegance and refinement, it's a setting worthy of a Dickens-era novel. For the most relaxed experience in this popular showplace, without the crowds the gingerbread house draws, visit during late evening and end your day with a warming nightcap.

327. Disney's Contemporary Resort also features a large gingerbread scene, inspired by famed Disney artist Mary Blair, best known for designing the childlike figures in Magic Kingdom's "it's a small world" attraction. The BoardWalk Inn has a different gingerbread construction each year, and the Beach Club Resort delights with its gigantic edible carousel featuring lots of "hidden Mickeys."

328. Humble woodland resort Fort Wilderness is the granddaddy of them all when it comes to down-home Christmas festivities. Along with the Golf Cart Parade, there are horse-drawn "sleigh" rides, and Santa shows up at Crockett's Tavern from 5 p.m. to 9 p.m. each Christmas Eve. The best part is, campers go all out with their holiday campsite decorations. If you're missing the decorations in your neighborhood back home, a visit to Fort Wilderness will set your mood right again.

329.
Camping at Fort Wilderness

The least expensive way to stay on-site and still enjoy all the perks is to reserve a tent camping site at Fort Wilderness, but campers who have not experienced Florida's outdoors may not be prepared for three contingencies: heat, humidity, and torrential rain. Bring extension cords, and hook up two fans inside your tent: one to blow air in, and one to blow air out. Extra tarps are necessary, especially in summer when afternoon thunderstorms are a near-daily event. Secure them to your tent with binder clips to help foil thunderstorm winds, or string them between trees to deflect heat. Then, line the inside of your tent with your ground cloth rather than using it outside, to keep pooled water from soaking into your living space.

330.
Pro Alert: Know Your MagicBand Purchase Limits

Guests staying at a Disney resort can link their credit card to their MagicBand and make purchases by tapping their band on a special scanner. But there are limits to how much can be spent each day. If you are reaching your daily limit of $1,500 at Value and Moderate resorts, or $2,000 at Deluxe resorts, you have two choices: Stop by the resort's front desk and ask the Cast Member to move your MagicBand purchase total onto the credit card you have on file and reset the limit, or, if you're already touring and your MagicBand charge is rejected, ask the Cast Member to call your resort to reset the limit. The limit won't be raised, it will just be reset.

331.
Rent a Villa for a Large Group

Guests visiting Orlando with four or more kids, extended family, or friends, require an accommodation that will sleep more than five. Groups who don't have the budget for two or more rooms, or one of Disney's larger suites, will find the answer in a vacation villa. Orlando has a massive inventory of two- to twenty-three-bedroom short-term rental homes, and nearly all of them include a private pool. Full kitchens allow for inexpensive at-home meals, a full-sized washer and dryer mean lower luggage fees with your airline, and purchasing one less day on your Disney park tickets for a rest day at your villa can save hundreds for a family of five. Kissimmee vacation homes are near Disney; Highway 27 homes are twenty to thirty minutes away.

332.
Find the Unscheduled Meet-and-Greets

You can't get enough of the characters, but meet-and-greet wait times can be long in the theme parks, especially during peak seasons. During the Christmas and New Year's holidays, drop by the Disney resort concierge desks and ask about unscheduled meet-and-greets that take place at the Deluxe hotels on some evenings, with the added benefit of the resort's outstanding Christmas decorations. Enduring a rare one-day park closing during hurricane season? Characters often drop by the resorts to help pass the time. No "special circumstances" during your stay? Wait times at Animal Kingdom tend to be shorter than at Magic Kingdom.

333.
Uncover "Hidden" Discounts

When is a Disney resort not a Disney resort? When it's the Swan and Dolphin Resorts, both of which are located on-site and enjoy many of the benefits afforded the official resorts, such as bonus park hours. However, they are not owned by Disney, and that's good news when it comes to "hidden" discounts. Parent company Marriott offers online discounts at www.swandolphin .com under "Special Offers." Florida residents and members of the American Automobile Association (AAA) have their own discounts, while members of the military can phone 800-227-1500 for current offers. Have a teacher or a nurse in your group? Inquire about discounts on the 800 number, using codes "Teach" or "Nurse." Firefighters, paramedics, and other medical personnel often receive discounts too.

Online Lost and Found

Whether you're still at Walt Disney World or you've already returned home, that important item you just realized is missing still has an excellent chance of being found. Visit Disney's online Lost and Found recovery system at www.chargerback.com/disneyworld and fill in the form with as many details as possible, including where the item was lost, if you know (it's okay if you don't). Then, you'll receive an email from Disney with a claim number, and a second email with an update on their search, or any questions they may have, within forty-eight hours. Don't despair. Lost items are often found!

334.
Make Room Requests

The best way to get the resort view you want is to book the correct category, but you can fine-tune your options with room requests. Make basic requests, such as a ground-floor room or a room near the transportation, during online check-in using My Disney Experience. For more specific requests, phone your resort directly at least ten days prior to arrival, and provide the name on your reservation, arrival and departure dates, reservation number, and your contact details, along with your two top-priority requests. Or, phone Disney Reservations prior to arrival at 407-560-2428 and ask to have your requests notated on your reservation. They will also notate requests at the time of booking if you book through Disney. Remember, these are requests, not guarantees.

335.
Schedule Garden Grocer Deliveries

Having groceries and basic necessities delivered directly to your resort is a real boon on arrival day, a time-saver over driving to a local grocery store, and a savings in comparison to shopping in Disney's convenience outlets. Guests who use paid-for transportation from the airport rather than renting a car have limited options, and Amazon Prime deliveries aren't available to non-members. That's where Garden Grocer steps in to fill the need. No need to pack bulky items such as diapers, soda, or cereal. Need kosher or organic? You're covered. Download the Garden Grocer app, place your order, pay your purchase amount and a delivery fee, and they'll deliver to your resort's Bell Services. Ages twenty-one and up can order beer and wine, including local craft brews.

336.
Room Check Before Unpacking

Immediately after entering your room, make sure the heat or air conditioning is working, the bathroom has hot water, and the shower's water pressure is good. Politely report problems to the front desk, a manager, or Mousekeeping, and ask for the issue to be addressed. While larger issues may not be corrected immediately, you'll have greater leverage when asking for a move to a new room, or an upgrade. Once you're settled, check the clock's alarm if there is one. Just because the people before you wanted to get up at 5 a.m. doesn't mean you have to. This also saves you from the joker who set the alarm's volume up to rock concert–level as his personal gift to the room's next occupant.

337.
Set Up a Command Center

Running out the door for a fun-filled day is the surest way to leave something behind. Make certain you have everything you need before departing by designating one flat surface in your room, ideally near an electrical outlet, as your "command center," and make a hard-and-fast rule that this is where everyone will keep the essentials you'll use, whether it's for time in the theme parks, a visit to Disney Springs, or just popping out for dinner. As soon as you return to your room, put the loose items you use every day, such as tickets or MagicBands, car keys, wallets, and cell phones, on the command center. Before bed, add refilled backpacks or bags to the pile. Nothing gets left behind!

338.
Kid-Proof with Bath Towels

While children should never be left unattended in a hotel room, there are a few ways to make your room kid-friendly, and they're as easy as having extra bath towels on hand. Young children will have surer footing on a slippery tub bottom when you bathe them if you place a bath towel in the tub first. Rolled-up towels along each side of the bed can act as bedrails during impromptu naps when you slip them under the bottom sheet and tuck it in tightly. Putting two children in the same bed? Place those rolled-up towels down the middle of the bed for "my side, your side." Then, muffle hallway noise with a rolled-up towel stuffed along the bottom of the room's door for a quieter night's sleep.

CHAPTER 8

EATING AROUND THE WORLD

339.
Use Quick-Service Credits As Snack Credits

EPCOT hosts four festivals each year that include food- and drink-sampling kiosks (Food & Wine, Flower & Garden, Festival of the Arts, and Festival of the Holidays), and you can easily assemble a full meal by using your snack credits as you wander around World Showcase. The added bonus is, you'll get even better value from each credit by ordering samples costing $7 or more. You can also use your Quick-Service credits at the kiosks, but each person must choose all of his or her samples from a single kiosk. Choose as many kiosks as you have people in your group and order individually so you're not stuck with just one kiosk's cuisine. It's perfectly fine to swap with each other once you receive your items.

340.
Order "Burger Only"

Although you won't see it on any quick-service menu, you *can* get a hamburger without premium toppings such as cheese or bacon. Simply ask for a burger without these items when you place your order and you'll save $1 to $2 on the posted price. If you don't want the "extras" but would still like the standard toppings of pickles, lettuce, and tomato, make those requests known to the cashier before they ring up the order. You can also save $1.50 to $2 by asking for an entrée (such as a burger, chicken strips, sandwich, or hot dog) without French fries, baked beans, or other sides included as part of a meal platter.

341.
Use the Mobile Order Service App

Why wait when you could order food using the My Disney Experience app and bypass the line? Tap on "Dining," choose a counter-service location that accepts mobile ordering, tap "Order Food," then select the items you want and pay using your credit or debit card, or the Disney Dining Plan. Rather than waiting until you actually arrive at the restaurant, tap "I'm Here, Prepare My Order" on the app as soon as you're within range and the prompt pops up on your screen, so that your food is ready when you walk into the restaurant. Otherwise, Cast Members will only start preparing it once you're there. Be sure to check your order for accuracy when you pick it up.

342.
Order Before You're Hangry

On extra busy days, mobile order can get logjammed, and if you order when you're hungry, you may have a long wait. Instead, place mobile orders for lunch and dinner as soon as you enter the parks and just select later pick-up times. If something comes up, you can change the time (based on availability). Mobile ordering also has an "Available Now" feature that lists where you can pick up food immediately.

343.
Go Gluten-Friendly at Woody's Lunch Box

Woody's Lunch Box, the quick-service dining outlet in Toy Story Land, isn't just a cute, highly themed spot for Woody's toys (and honorary toys, which means you) to grab a bite to eat; it's also an ideal place to pick up a meal for guests who avoid gluten in their diets. Although the posted menu does not include special dietary options, each of the sandwiches can be prepared gluten-free just by asking when you order.

344.
Let Disney Make Dining Reservations

You've walked into a Disney-owned restaurant only to discover they have no tables available. Don't despair. You won't have to trudge all over the park to find an available dining time. Instead, ask the Cast Member at the host stand if they will book a reservation for you. Restaurant hosts have access to the online booking system, and are able to make reservations at any Disney-owned venue. Take note: Many restaurants within Walt Disney World are owned by third-party companies, including Yak & Yeti Restaurant and Rainforest Cafe at Animal Kingdom, and Tutto Italia Ristorante, Via Napoli Ristorante e Pizzeria, and La Hacienda de San Angel at EPCOT, while most of the Disney Springs restaurants and several at Disney's resorts are third party–owned and therefore not accessible via the system available to hosts.

345.
Newbie Alert: Speak to the Chef

Walt Disney World is the size of a small city, with a "population" to match, and with all those people visiting each day it's a certainty many will have special dining needs. Guests with allergies, including gluten and lactose, will find allergy-friendly menus at several on-site restaurants, and specially trained Cast Members can assist in making selections from the main menu. Low-sodium, low-fat, vegan, or vegetarian diets can also be accommodated. If a member of your group has specific dining needs, such as kosher, halal, or multiple-allergy, email Special.Diets@DisneyWorld .com fourteen days prior to dining, or phone Disney in advance at 407-WDW-DINE and arrange for special meals. Still unsure? The chef will be happy to discuss your needs table-side.

Fantasmic! Dining Package

Wait times for the nighttime show Fantasmic! at Hollywood Studios can be up to two hours in peak season, making the Fantasmic! Dining Package a tempting alternative. The package allows you to make a lunch or dinner reservation at Mama Melrose's Ristorante Italiano, 50's Prime Time Café, Sci-Fi Dine-In Theater Restaurant, or The Hollywood Brown Derby, or breakfast, lunch, or dinner at Hollywood & Vine. Diners choose one entrée, and one appetizer or dessert (or the buffet at Hollywood & Vine), and are given a voucher for guaranteed seating. Park admission is required. You'll save time, but it will cost a family of four as much as $250, depending on the restaurant they choose.

346.
Take a Rain Check

Not all of the amphitheater rows set aside for the Fantasmic! Dining Package are the best seats in the house. Some are in the splash zone, and they're susceptible to thick wafts of smoke when the wind picks up, so aim for the back rows. Also consider Orlando's famous summertime electrical storms before booking. The show won't run if there is lightning in the area, so that meal you purchased for the special viewing, and to avoid waiting in the queue for an hour or more, won't pay off. If you purchased the package and the show is canceled, return to the restaurant where you dined, or visit Guest Services, and request a rain check for access to the seating area on a less inclement night.

347.
Make an Instant Doggie Bag

Guests on the Disney Dining Plan often can't finish a meal. Youngsters are notorious for leaving most of their meal on the plate when they're hot, tired, overstimulated, or they just want to get straight back out to the fun. And theme park meals tend to be enormous, even for adults. Ziploc bags become ready-made doggie bags for nonperishable items, such as rolls, Mickey Waffles, chips, fruit cups, gelatin, desserts in covered containers, or cookies. It's not okay to stuff the bag full at a buffet, but it's perfectly fine to take leftovers from an à la carte meal. Be sure your to-go item won't melt or go rancid in the heat, and stick a plastic spoon in the bag for items that require scooping. Forgot your Ziploc bag or saving an item that might get crushed? Place it in a plastic cup and snap on a lid (many Disney dining locations no longer offer lids, but in-park Starbucks do).

348.
Score Last-Minute Dining Reservations

It isn't always possible to book dining 180 days in advance, and often the hard-to-get restaurants are gone within minutes of the reservations system opening each day. However, that 180-day requirement can be your best friend when it comes to snagging a last-minute booking. Plans change, kids get tired, and no-shows occur, which means cancellations happen all the time and availability is fluid. If you can't get the restaurant you want, keep trying, even right up until the time you'd like to dine. You can inquire at the host stand or Guest Services, or use your My Disney Experience app, and as a last-ditch effort for Disney Springs restaurants, try for an online booking through www.opentable.com.

349.
Seek Out the Quick and Healthy Meals and Snacks

Once upon a time, snack options at Disney were all about popcorn, cotton candy, and other sugary, salty, or fatty treats. Those days are long gone, and guests who prefer quick but healthy snacks and meals now enjoy the luxury of choice. Look for Disney Check items, which include food and drinks that meet the Disney Nutrition Guideline Criteria, indicated by a green check mark inside a yellow Mickey head on select dining location menus.

350.
Go Vegetarian at Disney

Almost every dining location at Disney offers at least one meat-free or plant-based option, but some restaurants are more vegetarian- and vegan-friendly than others with their dedicated vegetarian menus, and all can accommodate special diets upon request. Those who prefer to skip the boring green salad and enjoy hearty and creative dishes will find plenty of choice at Jungle Navigation Co. LTD Skipper Canteen in Magic Kingdom; Sunshine Seasons, Via Napoli, and Space 220 in EPCOT; Mama Melrose's Ristorante Italiano at Hollywood Studios; Tiffins Restaurant's and Tusker House Restaurant's buffets, and Satu'li Canteen in Animal Kingdom; plus Boma–Flavors of Africa at Animal Kingdom Lodge, Ale & Compass Restaurant at the Yacht Club Resort, and Blaze Fast-Fire'd Pizza at Disney Springs. Need something sweet? Erin McKenna's specializes in vegan cakes and pastries.

351.
Pause Before Booking Character Meals

Before you schedule a dining time at a character breakfast, stop for a moment and consider your priorities. Meeting your favorite Disney pals will probably be your main reason for booking, but the time of day you select is important too. Do you want to get a jump on the crowds at the attractions? Get the earliest booking time possible, ideally before park opening, especially if you're riding a popular attraction such as Seven Dwarfs Mine Train, Slinky Dog Dash, Star Wars: Galaxy's Edge attractions, or Avatar Flight of Passage without a Genie+ time or Individual Lightning Lane reservation. Is maximum interaction time with the characters your top priority? You'll receive lots of extra attention during the last hour of breakfast, as most diners will have gone off to the attractions.

352.
Devour Dole Whips Without the Wait

Fan-favorite Dole Whips at Aloha Isle in Magic Kingdom's Adventureland are deliciously cooling in the heat of summer and pure Disney comfort food in winter, but their popularity means you're going to be standing in a long, hot line waiting for that coveted pineapple swirl, and that's no fun. Instead, pick some up at the Polynesian Village Resort's Pineapple Lanai or Animal Kingdom's Tamu Tamu Refreshments quick-service windows. Fewer guests know they sell Dole Whips. Go one better and grab a shady spot in close proximity to Aloha Isle, place your order on the mobile ordering app, tap "I'm Here, Prepare My Order," and simply walk up to the window a minute or two later, smiling smugly as you bypass that enormous, sweltering line.

353.
Book Dining Reservations in Reverse Order

It may be tempting to book your dining reservations according to the order of your vacation days, starting with your first day and working through each day consecutively, but if you're staying on-site, avoid the potential pitfalls that come with thinking of the calendar and instead book your dining reservations according to which restaurant reservations are the most difficult to get. If you need a specific date, try for that first, but if you can be flexible, look at times toward the end of your vacation for a better chance at getting a booking. Most guests make their reservations in order, giving you an advantage on dates further into your vacation. Remember to have your credit card with you when booking, to guarantee your reservation.

354.
Reserve Popular Dining Experiences When Staying Off-Site

If you're staying in an off-site accommodation you will have to reserve your table-service dining locations day by day, starting 180 days in advance of *each* day, so if a popular restaurant is crucial to your happiness, you're going to need a plan. Disney Dining opens at 7 a.m. by phone, but you'll get an hour's jump on the masses by reserving online. Log out of your My Disney Experience account before 6 a.m. Eastern Standard Time, 180 days before the day you will dine, then log back in to your account at exactly 6 a.m., have your credit card ready (it will not be charged, but is necessary to "guarantee" your reservation), click on the restaurant you want, and try for the time you'd like to dine.

Classic Foods You Must Not Miss

There are certain foods at Walt Disney World that are so popular they've gained their own cult followings. They include: Dole Whip pineapple soft serve (Frontierland, Magic Kingdom), Chocolate Tart with the Grey Stuff (Be Our Guest, Magic Kingdom), turkey legs and Mickey's Premium Ice Cream Bar (all parks), Tonga Toast (Polynesian Village Resort), Kitchen Sink (gigantic sundae at Beach Club Resort), Mickey Waffles (all resorts), cheddar cheese soup (Le Cellier Steakhouse in Canada, EPCOT), and Zebra Dome cakes (Boma, Animal Kingdom Lodge). Don't miss them or you'll be awash with regret when you return home and your Disney-fanatic friends say, "Did you try the...?"

Find Grown-Up Dining Choices

Taste is relative, but timing and location are everything, and when it comes to dining, what works for families with children may not work for honeymooners or couples. With more than four hundred restaurants in kid-friendly Walt Disney World, how do adults choose the experiences they'll enjoy the most?

355. Couples deserve a date night, especially on vacation. When a restaurant full of kids just won't do, make a dinner reservation for 8:30 p.m. or later for a romantic date night or when you're visiting as a couple and want a peaceful meal. Most families have dined by then, although you may still encounter a few youngsters. Maximize your chances by choosing fine-dining restaurants such as Narcoossee's, Jiko–The Cooking Place, Monsieur Paul, Todd English's bluezoo, or Cítricos, which tend to have the fewest "stragglers" when it comes to kids. California Grill during Magic Kingdom's fireworks is the exception. Victoria & Albert's guarantees you'll dine child-free, but at a price point reflective of its exclusive Five-Diamond Award status.

356. Want a couple's dinner without the big meal? Opt for a lounge or a bar. Most serve food, often in smaller portions. Families are less likely to hang out in a lounge, providing a more grown-up atmosphere. Crew's Cup Lounge at the Yacht Club, Enchanted Rose at the Grand Floridian, Shula's Lounge at the Dolphin, and Territory Lounge at Wilderness Lodge are the least attractive lounges for families, making them ideal for couples. Looking for a bit of raucousness with your meal? Trader Sam's Grog Grotto at Polynesian Village becomes ages twenty-one and up after 8 p.m.

357. **Sip pre- or post-dinner drinks in laid-back style** at Belle Vue Lounge at the BoardWalk Inn, Il Mulino at the Swan, Outer Rim at the Contemporary, or the fabulous Nomad Lounge in Disney's Animal Kingdom.

358. **Some lounges are relatively family-friendly,** and that's good news for weary adults looking for a light sedative at the end of the day without having to leave the kids with an in-room babysitter. Try AbracadaBar at the BoardWalk; the Front Porch at House of Blues, Rainforest Cafe's Lava Lounge, or Jock Lindsey's Hangar Bar in Disney Springs; Scat Cat's Club at Port Orleans–French Quarter; Victoria Falls Lounge at Animal Kingdom Lodge; or Trader Sam's Grog Grotto at Polynesian Village (but not after 8 p.m.).

359.
Lady and Tramp Autographs

Lady and Tramp, from the 1955 animated classic movie *Lady and the Tramp*, are not walk-around characters, but you can still get their "autographs" just by asking a Cast Member at Tony's Town Square Restaurant in Magic Kingdom. The lovable pups are happy to "sign" your autograph book or other item on which you are collecting character signatures. Don't have anything to sign? Ask anyway, and wait for the magic to happen. You don't have to dine at Tony's to collect their signatures. Just make a polite request. Celebrating a birthday, anniversary, or other occasion? Put a word in your server's ear, or quietly inform a host or hostess at Tony's Town Square, and ask if Lady and Tramp could add a message to their autographs.

360.
Let Kids Loose in the Paleo Zone Playground

You didn't make a reservation for kid-favorite T-REX at Disney Springs, or perhaps it was a last-minute dining choice. Whatever the reason, you're now standing in the heat or the rain enduring the restaurant's long walk-up wait for a table. Rather than hanging around out front looking dejected, head straight through the gift shop to The Paleo Zone and put budding paleontologists to work. The covered dig site just outside the gift shop has dinosaur fossils youngsters can "excavate," gems to mine for, and geodes to split, and it's all for free. The sand isn't sticky, and the excavation tools are paint brushes, so even toddlers can join in the fun. There is a handy sink for washing up before heading in for a meal.

361.
Divide Your Big Group

You're visiting Walt Disney World with a group of six or more, but no matter how early you get up to start looking, and how diligent you are about checking and rechecking for a time slot at the restaurant of your choice, there is simply no availability. Whether you're nearing your travel date or you just want to get that booking made, it's time to work the system. Instead of looking for a group of six or more, try splitting your large group into smaller groups and search for tables for two or four rather than six, eight, or more. If you would like to request tables near each other you will have to call Disney Dining at 407-WDW-DINE rather than booking online.

362.
Check Receipts for Discounts

You've just enjoyed a Disney Springs dining location, or made a purchase at one of the stores, and the first thing you did was either crumple up the receipt and throw it away or toss it in the bottom of your bag, never to be seen again. But hang on a minute; you could be missing out on a bit of magic. Before you stash it or trash it, take a closer look at that receipt. Occasionally, you'll find a discount offer printed on it, toward savings on your next merchandise purchase. These discounts generally show up around Christmas, and they may come with terms of use, so be sure to check the coupon's expiration. It might only be valid for a few hours.

363.
Starbucks Rewards

Vacationing at Disney doesn't mean giving up your daily Starbucks. There are locations in each of the theme parks (look for the Starbucks logo, not the name), and two at Disney Springs. Happily, the outlets at Magic Kingdom and Hollywood Studios are located before the morning rope-drop holding area, so you can fuel up while waiting for park opening. You'll earn Reward points on purchases, but you can only redeem existing points at the Disney Springs locations. Using a Disney Dining Plan? Each drink only counts as one snack credit, so amp up your snack credit's value by creating the most flavor-filled drink you can, no extra charge per squirt. Don't forget the whipped cream, drizzle, and any sprinkles they're willing to pile on top!

364.
Accept the Food Challenge

Portions at Walt Disney World are enormous, so it's really saying something when a dish qualifies for the popular "man versus food" challenge. If you're among the many who seek out these massive meals while on vacation, try the gut-busting all-you-can-eat skillet, with five meats and three side dishes, at Whispering Canyon Cafe; or the astonishing forty-two-ounce Prime Tomahawk steak at Shula's in the Dolphin Resort, antacid not included. The gigantic Kitchen Sink at the Beaches & Cream Soda Shop is a rite of passage among Disney fans. It includes several scoops of five flavors of ice cream, every single topping in the shop, candy bar bits, whole brownies, whipped cream, hot fudge, and, of course, a dozen or more cherries on top.

365.
Newbie Alert:
Rainforest Cafe with Shorter Waits

Who doesn't want to dine amid a thunderstorm? Or under an erupting volcano? Or with a troop of gorillas going wild around them? Rainforest Cafe at Disney Springs has all that and more, but without a reservation, wait times can be prohibitive. Walt Disney World has not one, but two Rainforest Cafes, and the restaurant at the front of the Animal Kingdom theme park is always quieter. Because it is not located inside the park, you don't need an admission ticket. Just turn up and dine. If you plan to visit the park after your meal, skip the long front entry line to get in and exit the restaurant through the gift shop. There is a second entry, where your park admission will be scanned. Even if you're not dining at Rainforest Cafe, you can use this "secret entrance" to get into the park, but keep in mind it doesn't open until 8:30 a.m.

366.
Get Creative with Quick-Service Credits

You've been using your Disney Dining Plan for a few days and you just can't face another meal. Maybe you're saving your appetite for a big signature meal, dinner show, or character buffet dining. How do you make the most of your Quick-Service credits without putting your stomach in imminent danger of exploding? You already know your Quick-Service entrée credits can be used at EPCOT's festivals, but they can also be "split" into the equivalent of three snack credits, as long as the snacks are all deducted during the same transaction. That means you can get three bagged snacks to eat later, three scoops of popcorn for your group to split, or three ice creams to enjoy as you watch the nighttime fireworks.

367.
Drink at Oga's Without a Reservation

Oga's Cantina in the Star Wars: Galaxy's Edge area of Disney's Hollywood Studios is the hottest nightclub in the universe, or at least on the planet of Batuu. That often means reservations are hard to come by. If you weren't able to reserve a time prior to your arrival, wait until the last half-hour of the day, then drop by and ask if there is room for you and your group. Chances are the answer will be "Yes!" Under the My Disney Experience app's Check Dining Availability feature, you can click "Now" and join a walk-up list for Oga's (or other nearby dining locations) if available.

368.
Find the "Hidden" Menu Items

Tired of standard fare on the quick-service menus at the resorts, parks, or Disney Springs? Take note: Some offer a "secret menu." There are two ways to find out if a restaurant has items not displayed on their regular menu: Ask the Cast Member assisting you if there are any "off-menu" items, or check out the "Mobile Ordering" section of your My Disney Experience app. Under "My Plans," click on "Order Food," select the restaurant, and click "Order Food" again. If off-menu items are available, you'll see a section titled "Mobile Order Secret Menu." Make your selection and continue as per usual. You might also find non-menu items in the strangest places, such as "off-the-menu" cupcakes at Sprinkles bakery in Disney Springs.

369.
Multitask Online Dining Reservations

When making several dining reservations at once, open up as many browser windows as you have restaurant choices, click on one of your choices per window on Disney's online "Make Reservations" page, then log in to your My Disney Experience account. Once you're logged in, simply work through each one in order until you've secured all of your desired reservations. Make your first-choice restaurant the first window you'll open, and so on. Also try clicking the half-hour time slot you want rather than clicking "Breakfast," "Lunch," or "Dinner" in the "Check Availability" drop-down tab. You'll have a better chance of getting a reservation closest to the time you want if your exact time isn't available.

Mobile App Special Features

You've used your My Disney Experience mobile app to book Genie+, Individual Lightning Lane selections, and dining, but there are also less obvious elements that add next-level convenience. "My Resort Dashboard" stores your reservation details, including information on your resort and your room, as well as transportation system maps. You can even use it to call your resort's front desk. Lose your park map? It's on the app. Want to find a PhotoPass photographer or view your photos? That's on the app too. "Spotlights" point out interesting opportunities. Find everything from current wait times for the attractions to the location of the nearest restroom.

Disney Dining Plan

Dining can eat through your budget quickly at Walt Disney World and, with the convenience of tapping your MagicBand instead of pulling out your wallet, it's easy to forget about the bill that will come later. Disney's Dining Plans keep a lid on spending, and avoid unhappy surprises long after the last cupcake has been eaten.

370. Guests who book a vacation package with room and tickets, either online or through Disney (or room-only by calling Disney directly), can add one of two Dining Plans to their reservation, for use at more than 150 locations around Walt Disney World.

371. Each guest on the reservation must be on the same Dining Plan, it must be purchased for the duration of your stay, and ages three through nine must order from the children's menu. Meal "credits" (based on the number of days on your reservation) are loaded on to each guest's resort ID card or MagicBand, which a Cast Member at your chosen dining location will scan to redeem the appropriate number of credits. You will then receive a receipt showing how many credits your group has left, but keep in mind that meals are nontransferable between party members.

372. The quick-service Disney Dining Plan includes two meals (one entrée, one beverage) at quick-service or counter-service dining locations only, one snack (such as popcorn, fruit, ice cream, or a nonalcoholic beverage), and one refillable mug per guest. Beverage choices include alcohol for ages twenty-one and up.

373. One of the main joys of a Disney vacation for serious foodies is abundant access to excellent restaurants, in which case the Disney Dining Plan includes one table-service meal (one entrée, one beverage, and one dessert/

side salad/soup/fruit or one buffet at lunch or dinner), one quick-service or counter-service meal (one entrée, one beverage), one snack or nonalcoholic beverage, and one refillable mug per guest.

374. Want to give a signature dining restaurant a try? Two table-service credits can be redeemed for select signature dining, character dining, and dinner shows. Skip a table-service meal one day to cover the extra credit for signature dining, or split meals to save up credits. If adults split a counter-service meal at dinner twice, they'll have leftover table-service credits to cover signature dining.

375. Have children with hearty appetites? When you dine at a location that doesn't offer a children's menu, they can order off the regular menu.

Bear in mind, with the exception of dinner shows and Cinderella's Royal Table, gratuities are extra. Watch for Disney Dining Plan hacks for specific situations throughout this chapter.

376.
Find Smaller Meals for Smaller Appetites

Guests with light appetites may feel intimidated when confronted with the large portions served at most Disney restaurants, but fear not; you don't have to wade through a massive meal or throw away half of your food. Although signage at the quick-service restaurants indicates kids' meals are for ages nine and under, older kids and adults can order one even if they're not visiting with young children. Although kids' menu choices usually feature burgers, chicken nuggets, or macaroni and cheese, each comes with a side dish, dessert, and a small beverage. For variety, try Pecos Bill Tall Tale Inn and Cafe's nachos or rice bowl (Magic Kingdom), La Cantina's empanada (EPCOT), Woody's Lunch Box's turkey sandwich (Hollywood Studios), or Satu'li Canteen's wood-grilled chicken bowl or fried tofu (Animal Kingdom).

377.
Show Your Loyalty

Several restaurants at Walt Disney World are not owned by Disney, and that means special rewards for being a loyal customer. A month before your departure, sign up for Landry's Select Club at www.landrysselect.com for discounts on merchandise, points toward future dining, and a $25 gift certificate to use during your birth month. Although sign-up costs $25, you receive a credit for that amount within two days, so ultimately you break even. Landry's restaurants at Disney include Rainforest Cafe, T-REX, and Yak & Yeti. Other loyalty clubs include Earl of Sandwich at www.earlofsandwichusa.com/rewards and Sprinkles at www.sprinkles.com/perks. Not only will you receive coupons and points, you'll also get a free brownie from Earl of Sandwich and a free cupcake from Sprinkles on your birthday.

378.
Celebrate—with a Special Cake

You're already celebrating that "big event" in the most magical place on Earth, but what's a celebration without a cake? Standard and specialty cakes can be delivered to your Disney resort with twenty-four to forty-eight hours' notice by calling 407-827-2253, but what if you have dietary restrictions? Guests with gluten intolerance, vegans, and those who keep kosher will find scrumptious choices at Erin McKenna's Bakery NYC at Disney Springs. Allergies including soy, dairy, egg, and most nuts are accounted for, and the smallest cakes serve eight guests while the largest serve up to forty. Orders can be placed by phone at 407-938-9044. Not only that, but with seven days' advance notice they'll deliver your cake to any Disney-owned table-service restaurant. How's that for a happy surprise?

379.
Plan Ahead for Picky Eaters

From the humblest in-park kiosk to world-class, five-star dining, you're surrounded by food at Disney, but the picky eater in your group turns their nose up at everything. Avoid a food mutiny by knowing your options before you leave home. Check out the menus at https://disneyworld.disney.go.com/dining, and choose one or two locations in each park that appeal to everyone. Buffets are a good choice with fussy eaters, but the cost adds up quickly. Instead, seek out multi-option dining locations, such as Cosmic Ray's Starlight Café at Magic Kingdom, Sunshine Seasons in EPCOT, Sunset Ranch Market in Hollywood Studios, or Harambe Market in Animal Kingdom. Last-ditch effort? Ask to speak to the chef. Most table-service locations can modify a dish to suit finicky tastes.

380.
Newbie Alert: Find the Talking Trash Bin

You've just had a snack or a drink in the Odyssey Events Pavilion. Maybe you're sheltering there during a thunderstorm, you've filled your water bottle, or you've just used the nearby restrooms. Whatever the reason, you're in close proximity to one of EPCOT's most surprising and delightful "hidden gems." Want to look like a serious Disney pro? Seek out the trash bin next to the doorway across from the registers (it's the one that's plugged into the wall). Then, push the bin's flap open and listen. There's someone inside, and they've got something to say! Push a few more times for new commentary. This humorous talking trash bin is the last of its kind, so don't miss it. All of its "talking water fountain" cousins have gone silent.

381.
Take Part in a Small World Interaction

Select restaurants in the theme parks overlook attraction elements, such as the view into Living with the Land from Garden Grill Restaurant at EPCOT's The Land pavilion, Gran Fiesta Tour Starring The Three Caballeros from San Angel Inn Restaurante in EPCOT's Mexico pavilion, and the giant aquarium from Coral Reef at EPCOT's The Seas with Nemo & Friends pavilion. The classic attraction "it's a small world" can be seen from select tables inside Pinocchio Village Haus in Fantasyland at Magic Kingdom, and guests who are lucky enough to get a table next to the windows overlooking the ride will find large cards with funny "instructions," which can be used for a little interactive fun with the riders below. If you don't find them on the table, ask any Cast Member and they'll retrieve them for you.

382.
Indulge in Giant Cookies Without the Wait

Avoid the long queue for scrumptious baked goods at Gideon's Bakehouse in Disney Springs by visiting their original location at the East End Market. It's located at 3201 Corrine Drive in Orlando, and you'll find all the deliciousness of their massive specialty cookies there, with little or no wait.

383.
Keep Ice Cream Cold

The heat index has reached an alarming level, with humidity to match, and that means it's time for ice cream. Whether your preference is scooped or soft serve, the risk is the same: It's going to melt in record time and there's nothing you can do about it. Or is there? Thermal cups are called that for a reason, and if you have one you've brought into the park, or you're not shy about asking for a to-go hot beverage cup at a counter-service dining outlet, you're in luck. Scrape the majority of your ice cream into the cup, leaving just enough in the cone to enjoy first, and the cup's thermal properties will give you several extra minutes before you're holding ice cream soup. For even longer-lasting ice cream, fill a cup with ice from the self-service soda machines, and sit the ice cream–filled cup on top.

384.
Pro Alert: Eat Here, Not There

Sure, you enjoy the finer things in life, but your wallet is begging for relief from table-service prices. There are a few quick-service locations that offer the identical or paired-down version of popular menu items at a significant savings over table service. Purchase the fan-favorite Tonga Toast from Captain Cook's instead of Kona Cafe at the Polynesian Village Resort; fish and chips from the Yorkshire County Fish Shop instead of Rose & Crown Pub in EPCOT; spare ribs at Morimoto Asia Street Food instead of Morimoto Asia at Disney Springs; or spectacular Zebra Domes at The Mara instead of Boma at Animal Kingdom Lodge. Always check the quick-service menu before shelling out for a popular item when the quick-service is connected by its theme with a full-service restaurant.

385.
Choose Meal Times Wisely

You've made a list of restaurants you'd like to try, and your 180-day booking window is just around the corner. Before making those reservations, check out the lunch and dinner menu items and prices on https://disneyworld.disney.go.com/dining. Menu items are often similar, but lunch is cheaper. When booking a buffet, aim for the latest lunch time and linger until the buffet transitions to dinner. As long as there is no gap between the times lunch and dinner are served, you can enjoy any added dinner items, but at lunch pricing. Is meeting characters at the character buffets more important than the food served? Breakfast buffets are less expensive than lunch or dinner. Choose the latest breakfast time and linger until the buffet transitions to lunch.

386.
Take a Culinary Tour

Ever wonder how Disney's culinary team blends the art of cooking with, well, art? Take thirty minutes out of your afternoon during a break day from the theme parks and join one of two Culinary Tours at Disney's Animal Kingdom Lodge and Kidani Village. One includes both Jiko–The Cooking Place and Boma–Flavors of Africa and a second one is at Sanaa restaurant at Kidani Village. You don't have to be a guest at the resort, or even an on-site guest. Anyone can experience these fascinating guided tours, which explore the resort's superb collection of African art, and delve into the creation of the restaurants' signature dishes (including tasty samples). The tours run daily, all ages can attend, reservations are not required, and they're free (check with Animal Kingdom Lodge for tour times). Hungry after all that talk of food? Book a reservation and enjoy some of the most creative dishes on Disney property.

387.
Get a Discount with Landry's

Rainforest Cafe at Animal Kingdom and Disney Springs, and T-REX at Disney Springs, are popular restaurants, especially for families with younger children. Meals there can really add up, so if one or both are on your dining list, you're going to want a discount. Sam's Club and Costco often carry discounted Landry's gift cards, and several online merchants carry them as well, but don't just look for a card bearing the Landry's, Rainforest Cafe, or T-REX name. Both restaurants are owned by Landry's, Inc., which also owns McCormick & Schmick's, Morton's The Steakhouse, Chart House, and Joe's Crab Shack. All discounted gift cards from those locations can be used at Rainforest Cafe, T-REX, and Yak & Yeti Restaurant at Animal Kingdom.

CHAPTER 9

DISNEY WITH KIDS

388.
Use the Force

Jedi Training: Trials of the Temple may be gone at Disney's Hollywood Studios, but your dreams of becoming a Jedi are not lost. Jedi Master Justin Aldridge conducts unofficial, private training sessions at Walt Disney World resorts and other locations, where younglings (and adults) can learn the art of lightsaber battle to defeat the Dark Side. Find him on Facebook and Instagram as thejustinaldridge or email jbaldridge10@gmail.com to set up your journey toward mastering The Force.

389.
Save on Stroller Rental

Instead of wrestling with your child's stroller when it's time to board the airplane, or having it take up valuable trunk space in the car, purchase an inexpensive umbrella stroller at Walmart, Target, or Publix once you arrive in Orlando. The least expensive version is under $25, a savings of $80 over renting one at a theme park over the course of a seven-day vacation, and you will be able to use it beyond the theme parks, including at your resort, Disney Springs, and the BoardWalk. Then, when it's time to go home, gift your stroller to a family waiting to rent one, or donate it to a local charity.

390.
Counterbalance Your Stroller

You'll see it all day long in the parks: An excited kid jumps up from his umbrella stroller to rush into an attraction or meet a character, and the whole thing topples backward. Avoid constantly righting your stroller, losing your drinks, and looking like a novice by strapping Velcro-style ankle weights to the front wheels. They will keep the umbrella stroller balanced against the weight of any merchandise bags, backpacks, cup holders, or lanyards you're carrying on the back and will provide added stability over rougher pathways when you're visiting locations such as Fort Wilderness or Disney's BoardWalk Inn, where a few sections around the lake are actual wooden boardwalk.

391.
Give Kids a Cash Stash

Remember those M&M's Minis containers that work so well for carrying the coins you'll throw into a fountain? They're also a great option for giving young kids control over a set amount of money. Allow each child to decorate their own container before you leave home, and let them carry it while you're touring the parks. By giving them control over their allotment you'll prevent constant requests for more coins each time you pass a water feature.

392.
Pad Your Child's Ride

When renting a stroller at a theme park, bear in mind they are made of hard, formed plastic, they don't recline so your child can power nap, and, with only a single lap belt, they are not suitable for babies who are unable to sit upright. To add a bit of comfort, especially in summer when the plastic gets hot and children get sweaty, bring along a towel to use as padding. Bring a second towel and two large binder clips, attach the towel to the top of the stroller, and you've got instant shade or cozy darkness at nap-time. Remember, you only have to pay for stroller rentals once per day. If you plan to visit more than one park on the same day, save your stroller receipt from the first park, then show it to a stroller rental Cast Member at each subsequent park.

Calculate the Scare Factor for Children

Children can be frightened by nearly any attraction at Disney, as most are loud and fairly intense. While many scary rides are obvious, even some family attractions prove hair-raising for youngsters. Haunted Mansion is intentionally spooky, and its "stretch room" features shrieks, complete darkness, and a "hanged body." Mickey's PhilharMagic has an extended dark sequence; Walt Disney's Enchanted Tiki Room has aggressive chanting and a thunderstorm; and even the Tomorrowland Transit Authority PeopleMover goes through a dark tunnel. It's Tough to be a Bug! is utterly terrifying, and best avoided with kids under eight.

Still not sure if your child can handle a certain ride? My Disney Experience allows you to filter attractions by age, but also by "Thrill Factor," which includes drops, darkness, loudness, and the all-encompassing "Scary."

393.
Designate a Stroller Folder

Strollers must be folded before boarding buses, trams, or the train at Magic Kingdom, so assign one person in your group to be the "stroller folder," and have them practice collapsing the stroller as quickly as possible before you're surrounded by strangers who have no patience for frenzied fumbling with buttons and levers. It is a skill that will come in handy when everyone is rushing to board transportation. As a quick reminder when the pressure is on, place small stickers with each step's folding instructions (1: Pull; 2: Push/Fold) next to the appropriate mechanisms. This is also a major boon for grandparents who offer to take toddlers on the Walt Disney World Railroad while parents ride Space Mountain, and they can't remember how the stroller works.

394.
Prevent Pests

In spite of the human-made nature of the parks, there is still plenty of wildlife roaming around, and the birds and squirrels aren't exactly shy when it comes to stealing food from bags left in strollers while the family is enjoying an attraction. Theme park squirrels have infallible radar when it comes to unattended food, and they will happily chew a hole in mesh storage baskets or your cute Minnie Mouse bag. Keep snacks such as nuts, popcorn, dry cereal, or pretzels in doubled Ziploc bags to help foil their laser-sharp detection systems. While they can easily chew through it if they find it, the scent from unprotected food in the stroller next to yours makes it an easier target.

395.
Newbie Alert: Tag Your Stroller

Some things never change, including the post-attraction search for your stroller, especially if it's a Disney rental. There are dedicated "Stroller Parking" areas, but often the sign isn't obvious and guests simply leave their strollers near the attraction's entry. Cast Members move unattended strollers into the designated area, where it takes some doing to find your own—unless you mark it well. The majority will use a ribbon, bandana, or balloon, so go against the grain and purchase an extra-large, brightly colored luggage tag, write your last name on the insert card, and hang it from your stroller's handlebar. Disney provides paper name plates, but it's easier to spot an unusual luggage tag than it is to read all those names until you find your own.

396.
Start Slow with the Characters

No matter how many times you've been to Walt Disney World, seeing it through the eyes of a child you love adds a level of magic you may never have thought possible. To keep it that way, avoid booking a character meal for your first day. Instead, see how the child reacts to characters in the parks before splurging on an experience that might just make them freak out—or worse, go stone-cold silent. Introduce them to face characters first. They're easier for kids to relate to than a gigantic Tigger with a massive head, or a Goofy who seems larger than an oak tree. Good choices are Mary Poppins, Alice from *Alice in Wonderland,* and Peter Pan, with his naturally kid-friendly demeanor.

Trick Out Your Stroller

Basic umbrella strollers rarely come with cup holders or storage baskets, but it's cheap and easy to add these necessary accessories.

397. **For a two-in-one cup holder and mini storage unit, purchase a lightweight, over-the-door shoe holder with grommets,** trim it down to two (or four) connected sections, and tie it to the stroller's handles, taking care that it's not so long that your knees will bump against it all day. If your stroller has a fabric storage unit but no cup holders, line the top back of the two-section shoe holder and the top of the storage unit with heavy-duty Velcro and stick the shoe holder to the inside of the storage unit.

398. **For an ultra-easy storage and cup holder,** hang a reusable four- or six-slot wine tote across the stroller handles for quick access to drinks, sippy cups, cell phones, and other necessities. Local wine shops occasionally give them away for free. Just remember to take valuables with you when you enter an attraction.

399. **Large carabiners, also known as D-rings (those metal loops with spring-loaded openings),** make terrific bag and backpack holders when clipped onto your stroller's handlebar. String your reusable cups or water bottles with handles, your misters, or a stash of ponytail holders on them if you don't have a storage unit on your stroller. You can even carry your sleeping child's plush toy by stringing a carabiner through the manufacturer's tag.

400. Want to be admired by every parent in the parks? Look for large "stroller hooks" (carabiners) shaped like Mickey Mouse's head, online or at some Target stores.

401. Pick up a small, washable cosmetic bag or pencil pouch with a zipper and a strap and use it to carry pacifiers. Hang it on your carabiner with a spare pacifier or two in case you forget one in the early morning rush, or it goes missing during the day. It's easy to lose a dropped pacifier in a crowded park.

402.
Darth Vader Doesn't Love Children

Think twice about having young children meet Darth Vader, Kylo Ren, or Darth Maul on their own. They are intimidating bad guys with evil mindsets, and Disney is all about staying in character. Darth, Kylo, and Maul are not going to give your child a hug; they're going to give them serious attitude of the galactically unfriendly kind, even if they're facing down a five-year-old girl with sparkly pink Mouse Ears and a loving smile. Because that's the kind of guys they are. While onlookers will get a laugh out of their utter disdain for children, if your youngster insists on meeting these villains alone, practice some cool Jedi skills they can show off during their meet-and-greet. They'll get a much better interaction.

403.
Cope with Turbo Toilets

Few things terrify young children more than the self-flushing turbo toilets you'll encounter in nearly every Disney restroom. They sound like jet engines and they have a habit of going off while you're sitting on them. Even worse, they suck everything down with the force of a hurricane, and your preschooler will assume they're going down too. To avoid a tearful demand that they be allowed to wear Pull-Ups, calmly tell your children about them in advance and assure them you'll cover the commode's sensor. Sticky notes are a tried-and-true method, but if you're caught without them, simply cover the sensor with wadded-up toilet paper. Worst-case scenario? Put your hand firmly over the sensor until the deed is done and your child has exited the stall.

404.
Get a Celebration Pin for a Happy Reunion

Many parents' biggest worry when planning a Disney vacation is that their child will get lost in the parks' chaotic crowds. There are several time-tested ways of tagging a child with contact information, including pinning a laminated, homemade card to the back of their shirt (with their information facing inward), or attaching a luggage tag to their belt loop. But it's more fun to get a free "I'm Celebrating" button at Guest Services (Town Hall in Magic Kingdom) and use the Cast Member's marker pen to write your cell phone number on the inside of the button. Instruct young children to flip it over for the Cast Member who finds them, so they can phone you up and ensure a quick and happy reunion.

405.
Give Your Kid a Temporary "Tattoo"

Big kids sometimes get lost, too, and even verbal children old enough to have memorized your cell phone number may not be able to recite it when they're scared and upset. Give yourself—and them—added peace of mind by writing your cell phone number on the inside of their wrist (along with their first name, if they're nonverbal) using a skin-safe marker. Wait a minute or two for the ink to dry, then paint over it with a liquid bandage such as New-Skin or Skin Shield. The "tattoo" will last for four or five days, it's flexible, and it's even waterproof. If your child has an allergy, include that information on their wrist as well.

406.
Keep Contact Info "On Hand"

A colorful way to keep contact info "on hand" is by ordering small, personalized nylon pet collars kids can wear on their wrists. Your last name and cell number can be embroidered right into the fabric (it's safer not to include kids' first names), and they're waterproof, so no chance of info washing away on water rides or in swimming pools. These are also great for stuffed animals, so they can be returned if they decide to explore the parks on their own or go missing.

407.
Photograph Potential Souvenirs

Kids live in the moment, and never more so than when they're clamoring for souvenirs. Instead of purchasing the first thing they insist they can't live without, take a photograph of it—and of each item they ask for after that—along with a photo of the shop you found it in, and show them the series of pictures at the end of the day or the end of your trip. Allow them to select the one they still want, but bear in mind that while Disney Springs carries many of the most popular souvenirs, if you shop at the end of the trip, you may have to reenter a park to find the exact item your child has chosen.

408.
Brush Up On the Classics

Many children are more familiar with modern Disney characters than they are with some of the characters from older stories, such as Horace Horsecollar and Clarabelle Cow. If that's the case with your youngsters, borrow some of the classic Disney books or movies from your library, watch them on the Disney Channel, or read Disney-themed Little Golden Books before your trip so that they're familiar with a wider range of characters. While you're watching their favorite Disney movies, encourage older kids to pay attention to some of the obscure or iconic moments in the action and come up with questions or comments around them that they can bring up with the characters during meet-and-greets in the parks.

Disney with a Baby on the Way

Vacationing while pregnant can feel daunting. Your commonsense daily routines apply, with a few Disney-specific tweaks. Start by searching Disney's "Accessibility & Advisories," on the Disney World Attractions website page (click the "All Filters" drop-down tab, then "Expectant Mothers Advisory") to find out which attractions have expectant mother restrictions. Restrictions are listed at attraction entries too. All-natural ginger candies such as Reed's or Gin Gins are not only good for settling motion-sick tummies; they're also great for morning sickness. Disney doesn't carry maternity clothing, so tuck an extra shirt into your bag for the inevitable drips that hit your baby-belly when eating. The most important things you can do? Rest when you need to, snack healthy, and stay well hydrated.

409.
Ride Early to Meet Height Requirements

Spine compression is a thing. If your child *just* makes height for an attraction they want to ride, be sure to head there as early in the day as possible. After walking around for several hours they may be a tiny bit under height, and those couple of centimeters may result in being turned away at rides they would have been tall enough for if they had ridden first thing in the morning. If your child barely squeaks into a certain height requirement and there are several attractions within that requirement they are eager to try, make those rides your priority first thing in the morning to avoid unhappy questions about why it was "okay this morning but not okay tonight."

410.
Identify the Street Sweepers

When you first enter a theme park, take a moment to familiarize your children with the name tags worn by all Disney Cast Members. Point out the distinct shape and the color of the name tag, and instruct youngsters to approach a person wearing that name tag in the unlikely event that they get separated from you. Also help them identify "street sweeper" maintenance Cast Members. There are quite a few of them, and they wear identical costumes in every park: white pants or shorts, a white shirt with a Mickey Mouse patch on the front, and a name tag. They routinely intercept lost kids, and are among the few Cast Members who carry radio communication devices, so they're experts at facilitating a speedy reunion.

411.
Newbie Alert:
The Four O'Clock Meltdown Hour

When it happens—and it will—take comfort in knowing your child won't be the only one wailing like a tornado siren in the middle of Main Street, U.S.A. once midafternoon rolls around. Locals know it as the "Four O'Clock Meltdown Hour," and it happens every single day. Bear that in mind when the bellowing begins, and remember: Your kids are on sensory overload, they're probably dehydrated, and it's your cue they've had enough for the day. The best way to avoid a major meltdown is also the most obvious: Spend the morning enjoying the parks, leave after lunch for a nap or playtime in the pool, and return in the evening when crowds are lighter, the heat is subsiding, and attitudes have been happily adjusted.

412.
Never Lose Children's MagicBands

There are times when kids and MagicBands mix like oil and water. Some young guests believe they are sporting fine jewelry; others consider the bands a nuisance that should be flung to the ground at every possible opportunity. If your preschooler is dedicated to the idea of ditching their "it feels icky when it's wet" MagicBand, you can wear it for them or strap it to your backpack strap or belt loop. Make sure your children will wear their bands, including when they're wet, before you remove the tear-away portion to resize the strap from adult-sized down to child-sized.

413.
When Your Child Is Afraid of the Rides

It may be "the happiest place on Earth," but it's also scary, loud, and chaotic when you're a preschooler. To avoid a crying child who is unwilling to try anything once he's been frightened, start with outdoor attractions he can see, such as Swiss Family Treehouse, The Magic Carpets of Aladdin, and Beauty and the Beast–Live on Stage. Next, try bright indoor attractions such as Gran Fiesta Tour Starring The Three Caballeros and the Disney Junior show. As they gain confidence, move on to gentler dark rides like Na'vi River Journey and The Many Adventures of Winnie the Pooh. When it's time to try the likes of Haunted Mansion or Pirates of the Caribbean, equip them with a glow stick as their "superpower" to help vanquish the dark corners.

414.
Find Nap Spots for Babies

Can't get your infant or toddler to nap? Take them on the Tomorrowland Transit Authority PeopleMover in Magic Kingdom. The gentle movement soothes tired babies and sends them off to sleepy-town, Disney style. You can ride several times without exiting. Other good attractions for a nap are The Hall of Presidents, Walt Disney's Carousel of Progress, or Liberty Square Riverboat (when crowds are low) in Magic Kingdom; The American Adventure or the gardens at the United Kingdom pavilion (if the band isn't playing) at EPCOT; a quiet corner in Walt Disney Presents and a showing of the *Walt Disney: One Man's Dream* film tribute at Hollywood Studios; and Gorilla Falls Exploration Trail, Maharajah Jungle Trek, or Discovery Island Trails at Animal Kingdom.

Ready, Set, Pose!

Photo albums and scrapbooks all across the world are filled with Disney vacation pictures with everyone standing there, arms at their sides, looking awkward. Avoid boring photos by choosing a theme for your pose.

415. **If you're meeting a villain, act terrified.** If you're meeting your favorite character, pose with your hands clasped and gaze at them adoringly. Or go full-on ridiculous and ignore the character completely. Point at the sky; pretend you're deep in thought; or pose as if you're having a family discussion. The funnier you are—or the more serious—the better the results. Each person in your group can choose their own expression or pose, or choose one for the whole family. Pick a theme for the day, or for the duration of your stay. It's fun to look back at photos over the years and see how your ideas evolved.

416. **Posing with characters isn't the only way to give your photos an "I'm at Disney" feel.** The parks are exceptionally scenic, and you'll find props everywhere that will leave no doubt as to where the photo was taken.

417. **Have children sit down in the middle of Main Street, U.S.A., looking at the castle,** and take a photo of their backs in the foreground and Cinderella Castle in the background. In a few years, when the kids are grown, this type of photo will be among your most precious.

418. **Try aligning your hand, palm up,** so that it looks like you're holding Spaceship Earth in EPCOT or the Tree of Life in Animal Kingdom, and take a close-up shot.

419. Stand on the bridge between the United Kingdom and France pavilions in EPCOT, with the Eiffel Tower in the background, and line up the shot so it looks like you're picking the tower up with two fingers.

420. Make "binocular hands" with the Green Army Men in Toy Story Land; pose with a lamp post, *Singin' in the Rain*-style; or pretend you're pulling the sword from the stone or throwing a coin in the wishing well in Fantasyland.

421. PhotoPass photographers snap the same pictures all day, every day, and they love it when guests ham it up, as long as you do so quickly enough to avoid holding up the line, if there is one. Sometimes they'll even make suggestions, and you might get a few extra shots out of it, which is a big bonus if you've purchased Disney's Memory Maker digital photo package.

422.
Invest In Some Soft Earplugs

Children's ears are more sensitive than adult ears when it comes to loud noise, and unexpected sounds are even scarier when kids are overwhelmed, out of their element, or taken by surprise. Carry a few pairs of soft foam earplugs to smooth out the loud bang of the evening fireworks and the enhanced volume in shows and attractions. Simply twist the earplugs into a point, insert them in youngsters' ears, and they will expand to create a noise-softening seal. Soft foam earplugs are also terrific when it comes to canceling out most of the nighttime hotel room noise. They'll help sound-sensitive children drift off to sleep, and create a quieter sleep environment for adults without blocking important noises such as little voices and wake-up calls.

423.
Know the Stroller No-Go Zones

Although it is much easier to carry an infant in a strap-on baby carrier than it is to shift them in and out of a stroller when enjoying the attractions, and baby carriers are a boon when you need your hands free for other children, strollers are essential with children under age six. However, there are a few places where they're a hindrance or simply not allowed. Pandora–The World of Avatar and Star Wars: Galaxy's Edge are compact areas, making stroller navigation difficult. Leave your stroller in the specified parking area next to the last attraction you'll visit, have young children explore the area on foot, then pick it up again when you're ready to leave. Some pavilions in EPCOT don't allow strollers inside, nor do attractions, or many shops and restaurants.

424.
Get a "Stroller Used As Wheelchair" Tag— If You Need One

Disney's policy states that strollers are not allowed in the queues for rides, or in any of the shows, and there are designated "Stroller Parking" areas at or nearby the attractions. What about mobility issues and certain hidden disabilities that make a stroller necessary for visitors who are unable to use a wheelchair or electric conveyance vehicle (ECV)? In those cases, guests who rely on their stroller can stop in at Guest Relations in each of the theme parks and request a "Stroller Used As Wheelchair" tag, which will allow the child to remain in their stroller at all shows and attractions that accommodate a wheelchair or ECV. Cast Members are trained to recognize the red tag, and will direct you through the regular queue.

425.
Take the Kids to Mickey's Halloween Party

Once the sun sets, the parks take on a magical tone, especially during busy Mickey's Not-So-Scary Halloween Party. Dress kids in light-up shoes, which will help you keep track of them when they dart off toward an attraction or a trick-or-treat station. Additionally, attach glow bracelets to your stroller's handle to locate it easily in the dark. If you're attending Mickey's Halloween Party, bring along an empty bag or backpack to consolidate treats, and keep little hands (or big hands!) from dipping into their individual bags and scarfing the entire haul in one night. Youngsters are more likely to carry their own bag to each station if it's empty, instead of leaving it for an adult to lug around all night.

426.
Prioritize with Preschoolers

The way you tour the parks with preschoolers will be different than the way you tour with older children, or as adults. Prioritize your Genie+ choices, making slow-loading attractions such as Peter Pan's Flight, Enchanted Tales with Belle, and Tomorrowland Speedway your top selections. Concentrate on Fantasyland immediately after park opening, and don't underestimate EPCOT's gentle, non-frightening attractions. Have a child too young to visit Bibbidi Bobbidi Boutique? Opt for the "My First Haircut" package at Main Street, U.S.A.'s Harmony Barber Shop. And when your preschooler begs to ride Dumbo five times, do it. These years are fleeting, and Space Mountain will be there when you return.

Using Rider Switch

When one or more members of your group can't or won't ride an attraction, but can't be left alone, it's Rider Switch to the rescue! Ask the Cast Member at the attraction's entry if Rider Switch is available. If it is, one adult and any non-riders will be given a special card and directed to a waiting area while riders walk through the queue and board the ride. After their ride, the adult waiting with non-riders goes straight to the boarding area without queuing. Best part? One other guest can ride with them, even if they've already ridden.

427.
Find Events for Reluctant Volunteers

Some children love the attention that comes with being the volunteer at an attraction, other children would rather crawl under a rock than get up in front of a crowd, and then there are the reluctant-but-curious volunteers. Disney has three attractions with them in mind. Kids who want to participate but avoid being the center of attention can make their wish come true at Turtle Talk with Crush, where the supercool surfer dude takes questions from youngsters as they sit comfortably on a carpet. Attention-seekers can volunteer for a leading role in Enchanted Tales with Belle, while shy performers can simply join in parading around the room. And even the most bashful children tend to participate at Disney Junior.

428.
Request a High Chair Sling for Little Bottoms

All Walt Disney World table-service restaurants have high chairs for babies and children old enough to sit upright, but what about infants too young to sit unassisted? While babies are allowed to remain in their strollers in most counter-service restaurants, they must be held or transferred to a bucket-style infant seat or carrying-seat sling in full-service restaurants. These are available upon request. When dining at a counter-service location, a supply of high chairs will be available for guests to use as needed. Simply grab one and take it to your table. Dining alone with an infant or small child? Ask nicely and a Cast Member will carry your tray to your table so you're not juggling a stroller, high chair, baby, and your tray.

429.
Take a Daily Photo

Gather the whole family together each time you enter a theme park, hand your cell phone to the PhotoPass photographer stationed just beyond the entry scanners, and you'll end up with a lovely remembrance of each happy day spent in the parks. But you'll have a reminder of something else, too, and it could prove useful. Along with a tag, temporary tattoo, or other identification you've attached to children or nonverbal guests, the park entry photo you just took is a reminder of what they are wearing, making them easier to identify in a crowd, or in case they get lost. In panicky moments, you're not going to recall who was wearing what, and you'll have an instant reference tied to the park you're currently visiting. Another spot for a daily photo (and a handy reminder for the end of the day) is by the sign for the parking lot/area where you parked your rental car.

430.
Download Heads Up!

Disney trips mean a lot of time spent waiting, and that's tough on youngsters used to a fast-paced world. While many queues have interactive elements, and the best way to spend time together is talking, there are some waits that benefit from a bit more cerebral input, including that long wait you're enduring when you've staked out your parade or fireworks viewing spot an hour in advance. Download the Heads Up! app to your handheld device, and make it your end-of-day treat as you're waiting. Everyone takes turns holding it up to their forehead while other group members give hints about the word they see on the screen, and the holder has to guess the word. Family-friendly fun that makes the time pass quickly!

431.
Restaurant Survival Kit

Babies and toddlers aren't the most patient diners. Make restaurant time less stressful for everyone by assembling a survival kit so you're not digging around in a backpack for miscellaneous items, or worse, stuck without the necessities. Purchase a medium-sized, multisectioned bag with handles, which you can quickly grab out of the stroller at mealtimes. Pack it with a plastic bib (easy to wipe clean); baby or toddler cutlery; disposable hand and face wipes; a small plastic plate or bowl; enough disposable tray liners for the day's meals; and crackers or other nonperishable snacks. When dining at table-service restaurants, order any food items for toddlers right away to help avoid hungry tantrums. Happy baby means a relaxed meal for the family and other diners.

Family Locator

Disney parks are a great place to give older kids and teens some freedom. Time spent apart doesn't have to mean worried parents, though. There are several online companies that offer a "family locator" app, which, when downloaded to each phone, lets families or groups keep track of each other. You can also consult your service provider regarding the app they offer, and at what cost. Wi-Fi must be enabled and Location should be turned on for accurate results. Some locators only work on phones within the same network, but they offer peace of mind when kids venture off on their own.

432.
Underage Driver's License

There is something about driving a car that makes younger children agree to stand in the sun for an extended period, just for the chance to push the accelerator and turn the steering wheel. As a reward for the effort, a photo booth is located next to the exit for Magic Kingdom's Tomorrowland Speedway, where kids can get a nifty plastic driver's license, complete with photo. Adults who prefer not to shell out an additional fee have another option: Gently steer your little Mario Andretti away from the photo booth and ask a Cast Member at the attraction's entry for a free paper driver's license. Only the paid-for option is available at EPCOT's Test Track, so diversion tactics may be necessary in the gift shop.

433.
"Fire at Will!"

Kids have a natural affinity for games, and Buzz Lightyear's Space Ranger Spin is usually a big hit, offering the chance to take on the Evil Emperor Zurg and defend the universe. But what if you have a young child who can't quite add the "aim" to "ready, aim, fire," and they'll end up frustrated, or worse, taunted by older siblings? Never fear. They won't come away from it without a good score. Encourage them to "fire at will" as they ride. Each time they pull the trigger, or even if they hold the trigger down throughout the ride, they'll rack up points, regardless of whether or not they hit a target. They'll end up with a tidy score just for having made the effort.

434.
Bring the "Disney Smell" Home

It's been a fantastic vacation filled with magical sights, sounds, and smells. You've made memories to last a lifetime, and your first priority now that you're home is to book your next Disney vacation. While you're poring over your photographs, listening to your Disney playlist, and finding a special place in your home for your souvenirs, you can also add "smell" to your post-vacation reminiscing. Visit the Marketplace Co-Op in Disney Springs for Bowes Signature Soy Candles and pick up a supply of "the Disney resort lobby smell." You won't find it under that name, though. Look for "Clover World" candles, essential oil, soap, or wax melts, the scent Disney resorts use in their lobby diffusers. It's a magical Disney "welcome home"…until next time!

APPENDIX

MAPS

MAGIC KINGDOM

MAIN STREET, U.S.A.
1 ..... Walt Disney World Railroad
2 ..... Town Square Theater
3 ..... City Hall
4 ..... Harmony Barber Shop

ADVENTURELAND
5 ..... Swiss Family Treehouse
6 ..... Jungle Cruise
7 ..... The Magic Carpets of Aladdin
8 ..... Walt Disney's Enchanted
        Tiki Room
9 ..... Pirates of the Caribbean
10.... A Pirate's Adventure–
        Treasures of the Seven Seas

FRONTIERLAND
11 .... Country Bear Jamboree
12.... Tiana's Bayou Adventure
13.... Walt Disney World Railroad
14.... Big Thunder Mountain
        Railroad
15.... Tom Sawyer Island

LIBERTY SQUARE
16.... The Hall of Presidents
17.... Liberty Square Riverboat
18.... Haunted Mansion

FANTASYLAND
19.... "it's a smalll world"
20.... Peter Pan's Flight
21.... Mickey's PhilharMagic
22.... Prince Charming
        Regal Carrousel
23.... Princess Fairytale Hall
24.... Enchanted Tales with Belle
25.... Seven Dwarfs Mine Train
26.... The Many Adventures of
        Winnie the Pooh
27.... Fairytale Garden
28.... Mad Tea Party
29.... Under the Sea–
        Journey of The Little Mermaid
30.... Meet Ariel at Her Grotto
31.... Pete's Silly Sideshow
32.... Casey Jr. Splash 'N' Soak
        Station

33 ..Walt Disney World Railroad
34....The Barnstormer
35...Dumbo the Flying Elephant

TOMORROWLAND
36.... Tomorrowland Speedway
37.... Space Mountain
38 ...Astro Orbiter
39 ...Walt Disney's Carousel
        of Progress
40 ...Tomorrowland Transit
        Authority
41 ...Buzz Lightyear's Space
        Ranger Spin
42 ...Monsters, Inc. Laugh Floor
43 ...TRON Lightcycle/Run

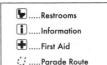

.....Restrooms
.....Information
.....First Aid
.....Parade Route

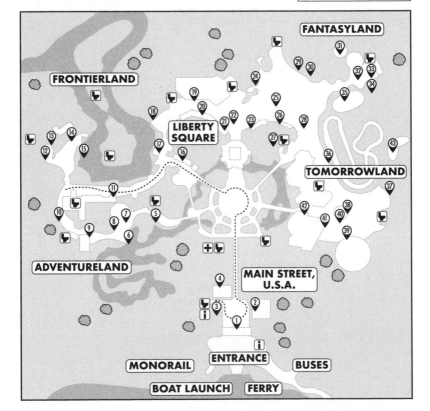

FANTASYLAND

FRONTIERLAND

LIBERTY SQUARE

TOMORROWLAND

ADVENTURELAND

MAIN STREET, U.S.A.

ENTRANCE

MONORAIL

BUSES

BOAT LAUNCH   FERRY

EPCOT

WORLD CELEBRATION
1 ..... Spaceship Earth
2 ..... Project Tomorrow
3 ..... Dreamer's Point
4 ..... Mickey & Friends
5 ..... CommuniCore Hall
6 ..... Journey Into Imagination
with Figment
7 ..... ImageWorks
8 ..... Disney & Pixar
Short Film Festival

WORLD NATURE
9 ..... The Seas with Nemo
& Friends
10 .... Turtle Talk with Crush
11 .... Living with the Land
12 .... Soarin' Around the World
13 .... Journey of Water,
Inspired by Moana

WORLD DISCOVERY
14 .... Mission Space
15 .... Advanced Training Lab
16 .... Test Track
17 .... Guardians of the Galaxy:
Cosmic Rewind

WORLD SHOWCASE
18 .... Canada
19 .... United Kingdom
20 ... International Gateway
21 .... France
22 ... Morocco
23 ... Japan
24 .... The American Adventure
25 ... Italy
26 ... Germany
27 .... China
28 ... Norway
29 ... Mexico
30 ... Nighttime Show

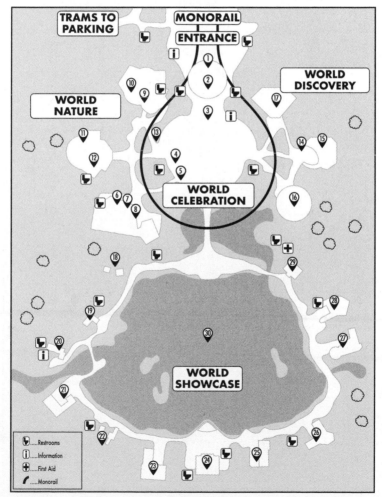

DISNEY'S HOLLYWOOD STUDIOS

ECHO LAKE
1 ..... For the First Time in Forever:
      A Frozen Sing-Along Celebration
2 ..... Indiana Jones: Epic Stunt Spectacular!
3 ..... Star Tours–The Adventures Continue

GRAND AVENUE
4 ..... Muppet*Vision 3D

TOY STORY LAND
5 ..... Alien Swirling Saucers
6 ..... Toy Story Mania!
7 ..... Slinky Dog Dash
8 ..... Roundup Rodeo BBQ

HOLLYWOOD BOULEVARD
9 ..... Mickey & Minnie's Runaway Railway

ANIMATION COURTYARD
10 .... Walt Disney Presents
11 .... Disney Junior

SUNSET BOULEVARD
12 .... Beauty and the Beast–Live on Stage
13 .... Rock 'n' Roller Coaster
14 .... Lightning McQueen's Racing Academy
15 .... The Twilight Zone Tower of Terror
16 .... Fantasmic!

STAR WARS: GALAXY'S EDGE
17 .... Star Wars: Rise of the Resistance
18 .... Millennium Falcon: Smugglers Run
19 .... Oga's Cantina

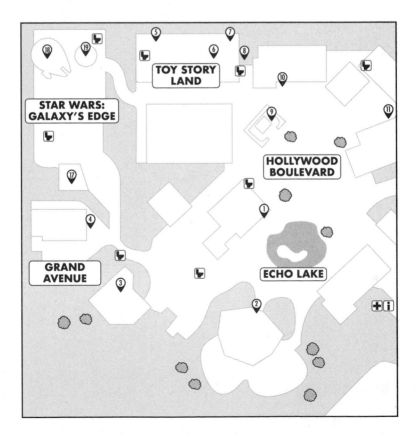

DISNEY'S HOLLYWOOD STUDIOS

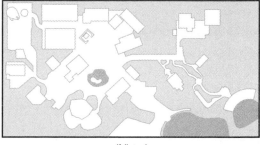

🚻	.....Restrooms
ℹ️	.....Information
➕	.....First Aid

(full view)

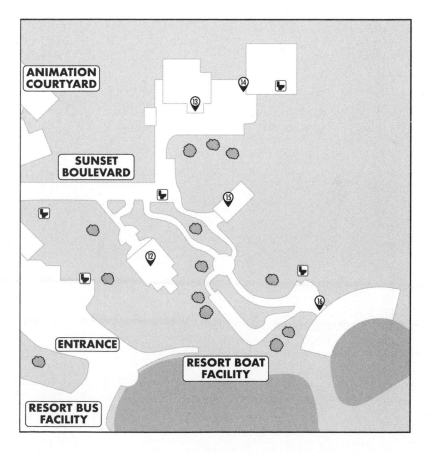

ANIMATION COURTYARD

SUNSET BOULEVARD

ENTRANCE

RESORT BOAT FACILITY

RESORT BUS FACILITY

DISNEY'S ANIMAL KINGDOM

OASIS
1 .....The Oasis Exhibits

PANDORA
2 .....Na'vi River Journey
3 .....Avatar Flight of Passage

DISCOVERY ISLAND
4 .....Wilderness Explorers
5 .....It's Tough to be a Bug!
6 .....Adventurers Outpost
7 .....Tree of Life
8 .....Discovery Island Trails

AFRICA
9 .....Festival of the Lion King
10....Kilimanjaro Safaris
11....Gorilla Falls Exploration Trail

ASIA
12....Feathered Friends in Flight
13....Maharajah Jungle Trek
14....Kali River Rapids
15....Expedition Everest

DINOLAND U.S.A.
16....Finding Nemo–
        The Big Blue... and Beyond!
17....The Boneyard
18....Fossil Fun Games
19....TriceraTop Spin
20 ...DINOSAUR

🚻 .....Restrooms
ℹ️ .....Information
➕ .....First Aid

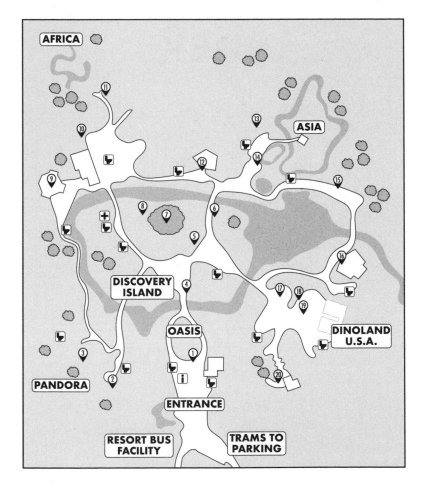

242

INDEX

practice using, 30
setting up and using, 22
special features, 202

Na'vi River Journey, 38, 72, 225, **242**
Nighttime Show (World Showcase), **239**
Noise
quiet spots, 122, 134
silencing fireworks, 136
Norway (World Showcase), 132, **239**

Oasis Exhibits, **242**
Off-season discounts, 34
Oga's Cantina, 201, **240**

Parades
Christmas Day (in November), 21
golf cart, at Fort Wilderness, 42
navigating during, 130
photo ops at, 141
Parking cars, 35, 36, 58, 63, 64, 77, 81
Parks. *See also* Attractions/rides;
Disney Genie+; *specific parks*
"Galactic Hero" status, 112
hopping between, 112
hours (regular and extended), 92,
170
navigating in single file, 115
quiet spots in, 122, 134
shortcuts between, 115
without a plan, 133
Pests, preventing, 215
Peter Pan's Flight, 73, 74, 150, 157,
238
Pete's Silly Sideshow, **238**
Phone
charging and extending charge, 12,
94, 97
creating lost phone photo, 87
lock screen, 87, 97
prepping, 31
using in the parks, 12

Photos
of admission tickets, 85
of airport parking location, 58
camera fixes, 89, 104
daily, 232
finding lost camera, 86
lost phone, 87
of marriage proposal, 98, 106
Memory Maker for, 48, 52, 54, 106,
147, 227
on-ride photos, 144–45, 147
at parades, 141
PhotoPass service studio, 52
PhotoPass use/tips, 48, 98, 134,
151, 169, 202, 227, 232
posing for, 226–27
of potential souvenirs, 221
spontaneous meet-and-greet, 142
of your schedule, 15
Picnics in parks, 51
Pins, Disney (real or fake), 41, 107
Pirate's Adventure–Treasures of the
Seven Seas, **238**
Pirates of the Caribbean, 73, 74, 225,
238
Planning your trip. *See also* Christmas
season; Schedule
about: general guidelines, 13
admission tickets (hard ticket or
eTicket), 26
calendar countdown, 27
clothes-folding and packing tips, 26
command center for, 182
creating Disney box to plan for
future trips, 19
"day three" phenomenon and, 19
Disney Genie system and (*See*
Disney Genie+)
doing parks without a plan, 133
dress code for Disney, 13
first day (park-free), 14
flexibility and, 20, 95

ABOUT THE
AUTHORS

Susan Veness is an international travel writer, researcher, and online content provider specializing in Florida, Disney, Orlando's theme parks, and cruising. She is the author of six books in The Hidden Magic of Walt Disney World series; she is also the coauthor of the *Brit Guide to Orlando* and the biography *Defying Expectations: Phil Rawlins and the Orlando City Soccer Story*. She has been visiting Walt Disney World since it opened in 1971 and continues to tour the parks on a regular basis.

Samantha Davis-Friedman was born and raised in southern California and spent ten years working in television production; however, her UCLA English degree was finally put to good use in 2011 when she began writing about family travel for *TravelAge West* magazine. Samantha currently covers theme parks for *TravelAge West*, *Family Getaways*, and *Attractions Magazine*, as well as the *MiceChat* and *L.A. Family Travel* websites. She enjoys visiting the parks with her two sons and sharing their adventures with readers.

THE MAGIC OF DISNEY—
IN YOUR KITCHEN!

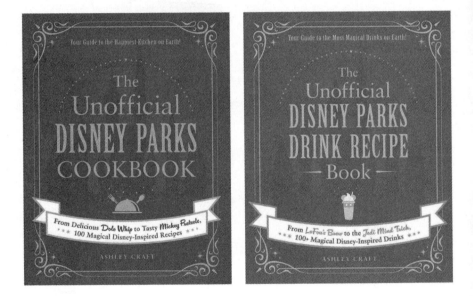

Pick Up or Download Your Copies Today!